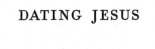

DATING JESUS

DATING JESUS

A Story of Fundamentalism,
Feminism, and the American Girl

SUSAN CAMPBELL

Beacon Press
Boston

Beacon Press
Boston, Massachusetts
www.beacon.org

Beacon Press books
are published under the auspices of
the Unitarian Universalist Association of Congregations.

20 19 18 17   8 7 6 5 4 3 2

This book is printed on acid-free paper that meets the uncoated paper
ANSI/NISO specifications for permanence as revised in 1992.

Text design by Yvonne Tsang at Wilsted & Taylor Publishing Services

Library of Congress Cataloging-in-Publication Data
Campbell, Susan
  Dating Jesus : a story of fundamentalism, feminism,
and the American girl / Susan Campbell.
      p. cm.
  Includes bibliographical references.
  ISBN-13: 978-0-8070-1072-3 (pbk : alk. paper)
  1. Christian biography—United States. 2. Campbell, Susan I. Title.

BR1725.C35A3 2009
277.3'0825092—dc22
  [B]   2009019341

Unless otherwise noted, all biblical quotes are from the New American Standard Bible.

To little girls and boys who ask tough questions.
You know who you are.

CONTENTS

THE DEVIL'S IN
AN AIR BUBBLE

The devil is in an air bubble floating beneath my baptismal robe.

This is troublesome, because I am trying to do the right thing—and, incidentally, avoid hellfire. I have walked to the front of my fundamentalist Christian church this Sunday morning to profess my love for Jesus and be buried with him in the baptismal grave. I will rise and walk anew, a new Christian, a good girl—not sinless, but perfect nevertheless.

But this damn bubble is getting in the way. It is Satan, come to thwart me.

I am a fundamentalist. I know that in order to spend eternity in heaven with Jesus, I must be immersed completely in the water, be it in a baptismal font, like this overly large bathtub-type model at the front of my church, or in the swimming pool at Green Valley Bible Camp, where I go every summer, or in a river, or anywhere where the water will cover me completely. I must be buried, figuratively speaking, because that is how Jesus did it with his cousin, John the Baptizer, in the river

Jordan.[1] It is how I want to do it now. I came to the earth sinless—not like Catholic babies, who, I'd been told, drag Adam's original sin around like a tail. Not me. Had I died at birth, I would have shot back to God in heaven like a rocket. But I did not die, and the time I've been on earth since my birth I've spent accumulating black blots on my soul, like cigarette burns in a gauze curtain.

And here Satan has floated up in a bubble beneath the thick white robe, and so I am not, technically speaking, completely immersed. My soul is encased in my body and my body is encased in this gown, and a small portion of it has swollen to break the water's surface, like a tiny pregnancy, or the beginning of a thought. My head is under. One hand is clenching my nose shut and the other is crossed over my chest, half the posture of a corpse in a casket. But if this dress doesn't sink with the rest of me, the whole ceremony will be useless.

I am a fundamentalist. We worry about such things.

A ceremonial joining-together only makes sense. I am thirteen when I decide to make it official. I'd been flirting with Jesus since age eight or so, the way a little girl will stand innocently next to her cutest uncle, will preen and dance for attention with only a dim idea of the greater weight of her actions. I meant no harm. I just loved Jesus. He made me feel happy.

In my mind, Jesus had been flirting back, and why wouldn't he? Our families were close. I went to his house three times a week, sat in his living room, listened to his stories, loudly sang songs to him. Our relationship was inevitable, and it seemed the simplest thing imaginable to declare my love.

And so on this bright and terrible Sunday morning I nerv-

---

1. For this and for all things fundamentalist, there is a scriptural reference. In this case, it's in, among other places, Matthew 3:13–16, in which Jesus went "up immediately from the water." See also Colossians 2:12, where we are "buried with him in baptism."

ously slide out of my pew to walk up the aisle during the invitation song, the tune we sing after the preacher gives his sermon. The invitation song is a time of relief for those who think the preacher has gone on too long, and a time of trepidation for the sinners who are paying attention. Although the song varies depending on who's leading the singing, all the invitation songs share a tone of exhortation firmly grounded in fear, meant to shake a few of the ungodly loose from the trees. And I am a sinner. I know that as assuredly as I know Jesus loves me. I am trying to live my life to meet the impossible ideal of perfection set for me exactly 1,972 years earlier by my boyfriend. The Bible said Don't lie, but I lie several times a day. The Bible said Don't steal, but I copied from a friend one morning in social studies because I hadn't taken the time to do my own homework. The Bible said not to lust, and while I am not clear what that means exactly, I harbor a deep and abiding crush on a series of pop culture icons from Bobby Sherman on—save for Donny Osmond, because he is too Mormon and I don't think I could convert him. But Donny is the only one from *Tiger Beat* magazine for whom I have no tingling feelings. I know, even though my church would frown on it because none of these boy-men are members, that if any of them save Donny drove up in a jacked-up Camaro and honked the horn, I would hop into the front seat without a look back.

Oh I sinned, all right.

As I begin to walk to the front pew of the sanctuary at Fourth and Forest church of Christ, I can hear the giggles and gasps from my girlfriends left behind. Most of them have already taken the walk to the front to declare their love for Jesus, but I have dragged my feet. I know I need to be baptized—it would sure beat spending eternity in hellfire—but it seems such an awesome step. I am walking toward the highest church office I can reach as a female—that of a baptized believer—and for that brief moment, all eyes are on me. I will be a Christian. I will teach Sunday school and participate in the odd rite of church dinners, where the mark of distinction is given to any woman who can assemble an ordinary-looking cake out of ingredients you wouldn't expect, like beer. Or potato chips. I will grow up and marry a deacon, the worker bees of our church, who will one day grow old—like, forty or so—and become an elder. I will raise up my children in the way they should go, and when they are old, they will not depart from me.[2] I will wear red lipstick and aprons and gather my grandchildren to my ample lap (all grandmas being fat). And finally, I will recline in my rose-scented deathbed with a brave, faint smile as my family gathers around me, and then I will rise in spirit to my home in glory, leaving behind a blessed bunch who look and sound and smell like me and who point to my faith as their ideal. They will, of course, all be Christians, and they will marry Christians and beget Christians, and not some watered-down namby-pamby type, either, but fire-breathing and soul-growing Christians, members of the church of Christ, saved by grace and fired with an obstinate belief in the black and white.

Give me that old-time religion! Yes, Lord![3]

It is all laid out for me, both in the Bible and in the talks our Sunday school teachers give us. I know my future as I know the St. Louis Cardinals lineup from the tinny transistor I sneak into my bed on game nights: Bob Gibson, Ted Simmons, Matty Alou, Lou Brock, José Cruz, and the man who will ultimately betray my faith in baseball and become a hated Yankee, Joe Torre. Those Cardinals will win the pennant one day, but I will be a Christian today.

The sanctuary in which I walk is a high-ceilinged, cavernous room covered completely—walls and ceiling—in knotty pine that

---

2. Proverbs 22:6.

3. But let's not get carried away. In fact, at my church, we don't raise our hands up to pray and we certainly don't cry out "Yes, Lord!" We sit properly and quietly, just as God intended. Let the Holiness crowd and the Pentecostals get loud. We're having none of it.

holds my secret sin. When I am bored—and during three-hour Sunday-morning services I am often bored—I attempt to count the knots in the panels behind the preacher. I lose count and start again, lose count and start again. I feel guilty about that, but I am sitting through three sermons a week and once I recognize the preacher's theme (sin, mercy, salvation), I start counting knots.

The room seats roughly seven hundred souls. I say roughly, because we never fill it. It was built amid much discussion and hard feelings at a time when my church was among the fastest-growing Christian groups in the country. Of course we would fill it, we told one another, even if our regular Sunday-morning attendance hovered around three hundred or so. God would provide. We just needed to have the right amount of pews. The interior looks as we imagine the ark of Noah would look—spare, with not one cross on display. Jesus hung on a real cross. Who were we to use the emblem of his shame as decor? And why would we, as girls, wear small golden crosses when the real one was so much bigger and uglier?[4] The pews are padded—another discussion—and there are no prayer benches, for fear that they would put us in company with the Catholics. Still, I never once saw someone drop to his or her knees during public prayer. We are, one visiting minister derided us, the only group of believers that sits to sing and stands to pray.

In fact, the building was built on prayer—and a painful schism. When you believe you are holy and have God on your side, you easily cross over into being dogmatic. We split over paving the parking lot. The anti-paving bunch argued that Jesus never walked on pavement, and that we shouldn't be so fine-haired as to worry about muddying our good shoes as we scrambled to our (padded) pews. And besides, the money could be used for a

---

4. This may have been an affectation of my own church, not the denomination in general. In fact, I would see girls from other churches of Christ with small, discreet gold crosses around their necks, and I would badly want one.

greater purpose—namely, saving souls. The grandparents of this crowd had cheered at the outcome of the Scopes Monkey Trial. Consider them opponents of creeping and sweeping modernity.

The other bunch—and, oddly, my notoriously hidebound family sided with them—said that paving a parking lot was right and good, that it didn't hurt to have a few creature comforts, and the anti-paving crowd hadn't kicked up a fuss over the fancy new air-conditioning, now, had they? When the church splits, we stay with the paved group. And when it splits another time over whether the grape juice of the Lord's Supper (the communion we enjoyed every Sunday) should come from one cup, as Jesus may have shared it, or from tiny shot glasses set into special circular trays made for such an event, my family again sides with the progressives. The others we derisively call "one-cuppers," as damning a phrase as "dumb-ass hillbilly."

It would be my family's one concession to change.

Among the literal-minded, schisms are just waiting to surface, ready to crack open at any moment. Elsewhere, the other churches of my faith—we had no central hierarchy, opting instead for home rule by a group of older men, the elders—would split and split again, over adding a pastoral counseling service, or a daycare center—more modernity, in other words, but that was later. For now, we felt the sheep were scattered, and when we brought them home, they could clatter across pavement to sit in padded pews and partake in the liquid part of the Lord's Supper from tiny shot glasses meant for just such a purpose—and likely to form a barrier against the common cold as well.

I may pass my parents as I walk up the aisle to my watery grave, but I probably don't. My stepfather—the one responsible for our membership here in the first place—likes the back pew, and my mother has headaches so she often needs to leave the services. She also volunteers in the nursery, a depository for unruly children who aren't old enough to count knots. My mother came late to fundamentalism, via my stepfather, her second husband.

He was raised in the church. My mother was raised by a stern couple who came north from Arkansas' Boston Mountains and trusted no organized entity, not banks and certainly not churches. For years they buried their money in mason jars out back, and they spent quiet Sunday mornings at home, reading the paper and arguing over which radio station to listen to. They were moral people, but they did not darken a church pew until after my grandfather's retirement from Atlas Chemical Co. Then they went whole hog and converted to Pentecostalism, and for years my grandfather's donations kept a little Pentecostal church's heat and lights on. But in her youth, my mother was responsible for getting her own self to church. More often than not, she met up with friends at the First Christian Church near her home in dusty little Carterville, Missouri. Despite the similarity in the names between her old church and her later one, the church of her youth was looser in its adherence to scriptural literalism, and so it, in the eyes of her new church, the church of Christ, hardly counted as church at all.

If my stepfather hugged the back pew, and my mother hid in the nursery, I usually sat up front in the right-hand corner with the rest of the youth group, a gaggle of fresh-faced teens and preteens who wanted so badly to do the right thing. We gathered there every service, saved places for one another, went for Cokes on the weekend. When we came of age we would be expected to date one another (if we were going to date anyone at all), which would, in the event, always have the feel of dating one's brother.

My close proximity to the front of the church makes my walk of shame (or triumph, depending on your point of view) infinitely shorter than it might have been. By the time I realize my heart is beating in my chest, I am already at the front row. A few deep-voiced men intone "Amen!" as I move. I think I hear my older brother in that group. He'd been baptized years before. I know he'll be happy for me that I've decided to spend my eternity in heaven, with him.

When I gain the first pew and sit down, an elder hands me a response card and a stubby pencil, and I scratch out that I want to be baptized—something everyone from my parents to my youth group has taken as a fait accompli. No one knows I count knots in the pine walls. That is my private sin. In public, I am Bible Bowl champion. I read my Bible on my own without anyone telling me to. My King James Version—and, later, my New International Version—is scored with pen and pencil underlines, and when I find a verse I particularly like (much of Proverbs, actually, and a great deal of Hebrews as well), I bear down so hard that I tear the page. Yes! Right on, God! It is a point of honor that I even mark a few verses in the rarely read book of Ezekiel, and when it comes time to gather with the other saved, I make sure to flash Ezekiel just to show them how serious I am. That, I think, marks me as a true biblical scholar: I even read the boring books—read them and find portions of them pertinent enough to underline. The better-read books I drink in. On several pages in Matthew and Mark, all but a few verses are underlined. On Judgment Day, I intend to wordlessly hand my marked-up Bible to God, and he will wave me into heaven.[5]

I go further than that. Unlike my lax fellows, I actually work my Sunday school lessons—in advance, and not in the car on the way to church, either. However much they let me do at church, I do. I sing alto in a youth group that travels around to old folks' homes. I work a puppet in a pretend gospel quartet that sings along to recorded hymns. I go to church camp every summer and sit beneath the stars on chilly nights to sing hymns by a campfire. I never once, as did my friends, glance around the glowing circle to imagine which of these short-haired young men will one day take me for a bride. I have bigger plans, although if you ask for

---

5. I grew up capitalizing any pronoun that referred to the Supreme Being. God was a He—or, in my private thoughts, a She. But we're bowing to style here and low-ercasing. May lightning not rain down on our heads.

specifics, I can't name any. I sign letters to the friends I make at church camp "In His Service," just like that, without a trace of irony. I vow to do a good deed every day, and several nights a month I sit up fast in bed realizing I'd forgotten, and that I'd disappointed Jesus. So I double up the next day. I set the bar impossibly high because Jesus died for my sins, and it seems the least I can do to pen a card to a shut-in, loan some lunch money, or plant a flower bed for a neighbor.

I memorize my Bible verses, memorize the books of the Bible (which, decades later, I can still say in record time, as if somewhere there's a hair comb with John 3:16 stamped on it waiting for me, my prize). When my church, like so many others in our area, starts a bus ministry, I will enthusiastically volunteer to be a teacher. I will take notes at the sermons and carefully navigate life at my secular high school, where it seems like everyone is drinking and having sex but me. I will try to draw my friends to the faith by my own fierce good example. I will not gossip. Any school activities scheduled on Sundays or Wednesday nights will have to count me out. I will be in church every time the doors are open. I will be the town virgin and it won't be a sacrifice, but, rather, a way to avoid the inevitable groping and pawing that scares me to death. I will, instead, date Jesus.

I am Jesus's and his alone, and I am pretty sure I am sincere.

I wish I could say I am motivated by love totally and entirely. I love Jesus, yes, but I also fear him. I fear his return for Judgment Day, when he will come like a thief in the night, when I most likely will be found not ready, and I will shoot straight to hell, my soul boring through the bedrock and limestone straight to the fires. I can't quite get my literalistic mind around how I can burn for eternity, so I settle on being stung by hornets, and that is bad enough. That, and the shame I imagine in my parents' eyes as I trudge off behind the devil. The sermons I half-listened to on Sunday morning, Sunday evening, and Wednesday evening all carry with them cautionary tales of not being ready, and how awful that would be, and how disappointed God. And we know not when it will happen. It could happen on a sunny day, a wintry day—although I tend to think it will happen during a particularly fierce summer thunderstorm. I am afraid of the thunder, and it seems a perfect venue in which to end the whole shebang, in one fell swoop scare the pants off of me and end the world at the same time.

This is southwest Missouri, the Ozarks, which rests comfortably in both the Bible Belt and Tornado Alley. I sometimes wonder if there is a correlation. If you spend your formative years driving by piles of sticks that a half hour before were homes and schools, you may be more inclined to believe in a vengeful, Old Testament God, the kind that can roll down from the hills and destroy your life with the flick of a wrist. Had I grown up in, say, Helena or Baltimore, would the threat have seemed so great?

No storm shelter can provide succor from that kind of power. If I am daily doing a good deed, I am doing so to earn, as the old hymn goes, "stars in my crown."[6] There will be an accounting and I want to be sure to have done a lot of nice things that will make God and His Son treat me favorably.

I have a picture of God in my head. He is a white man with a white beard in a white robe, holding a thunderbolt as if to throw it like a javelin. The picture is heavily influenced by a book I find in my grandmother's attic. With pictures and maps, the book explores ancient Greek and Roman gods. I am envisioning Zeus, but I never would have admitted that out loud. That book is a classic and I wish I could bring it home, but I leave it there at my grandmother's so that during interminably long visits, when the grownups are content to sip iced tea and talk, I have an escape. I like that

6. From a hymn written around the turn of the last century: "Will there be any stars, any stars in my crown? When at evening the sun goeth down?" (and the basses sing, "Goeth down").

book a great deal; the Greek and Roman goddesses carry a lot of weight, and they do that not because they are favored by some deity to bear a child, like God favored the Christian's Mary. They exist on their own steam, for their own reasons, and they have powers unique to them. Eventually I come across the notion of vestal virgins, and think I would be well suited for such a position. We fundamentalists don't have such offices for women. We have Ruth, known mostly for her willingness to throw over her own culture for that of her husband's family. And we have Esther, who is a beautiful queen who works it to help her people. I prefer the antics of Minerva, Artemis, or even Aphrodite, who doesn't appear to have a practical bone in her body. But she is smart and people worship her.

Nestled in a box next to the myth book is a worn copy of *The Children's Bible,* complete with pictures and easy-to-read text. It is the first Bible I encounter that is geared to my own age. When I am old enough, I am handed an onionskin-paged Bible just like my mother's, and I am expected to make sense of it without any pictures—if you don't count the multicolored maps in the back, and I don't.

In the children's Bible, the pictures of my Jesus show a wan-looking lemon-blond Swedish man, always with one finger pointed heavenward and a hand clasped to his chest, with the most unreadable face I'd ever seen. Is he angry? I am familiar with anger. Is he bemused? (This would have been a new word for me.) He looks more than anything like his mind is on something else, someplace far from the dusty streets of Nazareth. Honestly, with his flowing blond locks he looks more girlish than anything, but a careful reading of the Scriptures teaches you that turning water into wine is not much more than a party trick for Jesus. My Savior packs a punch. I am a big fan of his throwing the money changers out of the temple. The Son of God, with his notable connections, is capable of far, far more. And so Jesus is a boyfriend who drives a muscle car—say, a Charger—and has tattoos. He's gentle as a kitten most of the time, but you wouldn't want to cross him.

Back on the front row, I feel exposed. I confess on the response card that I have sinned—thankfully, a blanket confession of sin is sufficient; we aren't required to go into detail like the Catholics— and nice Mrs. Brackett—my sometime Sunday school teacher —takes me into a small room behind the pine wall at the front of our sanctuary—although we don't call it that. We don't call it anything, really. It is where we have church, and that is enough. I am given a heavy white robe that swallows me, and told quietly to remove my Sunday best. I fold my clothes and place them on a bronze-colored folding chair, and wonder for a moment what to do about my underwear. Wearing nothing beneath a white robe that is soon to be wet could be social suicide, so I decide to risk discomfort and keep them on. I cinch the robe's waist—later, when I don my first karate gi, I will feel the fabric's thick texture and be back in the baptistery. Mrs. Brackett pulls a curtain aside and I step into the chilly baptistery water, and am met from the other side by the smiling minister, a young man with too-longish hair (if you asked my parents), and his beautiful wife. He tells me softly to watch my step, and then I turn to stand with my back to him, as if he were hugging me from behind. To my right is a pastoral scene painted on—as I can see now that I am up close—a cheap piece of particleboard. A curtain that hangs between the baptistery and the congregation is noisily opened, and I stare into the water. No one has to tell me what to do. I have sat through countless such rituals. The minister raises one hand over us, says my name, and pronounces me buried with Christ, then I am dunked completely underwater because that is what we thought John the Baptizer did when Jesus came to him before he started his ministry. Sprinkling would not be good enough, because it would not emulate real-live burial and the point is to bury my old self and rise to walk anew.

But then the heavy white robe floats up on an air bubble as the nice minister is leaning me backward. I panic a moment and wonder if I should perhaps reach to smash it down. Would the baptism count if clothing remains above water? When you are raised a fundamentalist, the world turns on a literal axis, and nowhere is this more evident than in the few rituals we allow ourselves. The New Testament Scriptures carry no evidence of a piano being included in the worship services of the early church, and so we do not allow a piano—or an organ or trumpet or drum either. Years later, a friend of mine who is a member of the church will ask if she can wheel a piano in just for the duration of her wedding. She is told no. It isn't that the elders object to "The Wedding March." For us, weddings are not a sacrament, not a part of a worship service, and so if you want to have trained monkeys carry your ring in on a maypole, that would be fine as long as you clean up afterward. It is a very particular point of faith that keeps our leaders from allowing a baby grand to come inside. The elders worry that someone will drive by the church, see a piano going through our wide doors, and think that we have finally given in on this most important matter of faith.

"But can I bring it in under cover of darkness?" my friend asks.

No. The risk is simply too great. For years, my church had set itself apart by not allowing musical instruments in our worship, and now is no time to bend.

And so my friend is married at a local country club, where a piano is already a part of the decor. The elders would not budge, despite the fact that her father is a doctor and much loved by the fellowship. I sometimes wonder what would have happened if they'd allowed a piano to come inside our church and then discovered they liked it.

That literal axis would often cause me pause. We are taught not to capitalize "church" in "church of Christ," and to this day I know that someone's the real thing if they leave the *c* small. We are taught that women are to keep silent in the assembly, and so women are not allowed to talk in church at all. They can teach Bible classes, but not if there are any men in the room. The first time I hear a woman's voice over a public-address system at a religious function is at a Tulsa bus-ministry expo, and before the woman at the podium can speak, a man comes through and ushers out the door the handful of men who've inadvertently wandered in. Whatever the spiritual state of those men, they cannot hear a woman's voice over a PA if she is going to talk about God.

And there is my gown, floating up. I am worried about revealing my underwear to the minister but my main concern is whether this baptism counts. I try to think how I might signal to the minister that there is a problem, but before I can do anything, the bubble breaks, the robe sinks with me, and my spiritual crisis is averted. I rise to walk anew with my Lord, my Savior, my Jesus, to the amens of my newly acquired brothers in Christ. The sisters sit silent.

As I peel off the robe and dress back behind the baptistery, I wait for the enormity of what I've done to hit me. I will be surprised in the same way later, the first time I have sex. I had thought on both occasions that the event would be so huge that people around me would see how altered I was. Five minutes ago I was a sinner. And now? I'm a Christian. Five minutes ago I was a virgin. And now? I'm a—what?—woman? Harlot? Really pleased that I finally managed to hand over my virginity with as little fuss as possible?

At thirteen, you may not know a lot, but perhaps more than at any other time in your life, you know how to believe in something. You are capable of a faith that is deep and bedrock-firm. I had entered a fundamentalist Christian faith, a throwback to the days when people decried what they saw as the erosion of God's plan, pointing to symptoms like movie theaters, dancing, divorce, and promiscuous sex. But I was raised in the '60s and '70s and all of those things were already a part of the culture. We could no more deny them than we could the Vietnam War, where my dad was fighting, and so our faith was woefully out of step with the rest of the world. And that, given how we read the Bible, told us we were on to something. Early Christians were out of step with their world, too, were they not? We could take comfort that the rest of the world thought we were nuts. The farther afield we appeared, the closer to God we felt.

But the floating white robe weighed on my heart. I hadn't been open to the Spirit at that moment. I'd been worried about a little piece of fabric. Maybe I had not been in the proper mind frame. Why else would I feel so small while all my friends and many of the adults in the church gathered around to congratulate me afterward? Why did I only shiver at the feel of my wet underwear against my skin? Where is the fear and trembling I'd been taught to expect?

When the crowd that has gathered to congratulate me disperses, I climb into the backseat of my family's car—for once acquiring a window seat without having to argue for it with my two older brothers—and ride to McDonald's for a celebratory meal. While everyone chatters around me, I wait to feel something— the dove descend, the earth open up—but I feel nothing.

I ponder that through a few more thunderstorms, and then, a few months later, certain that I haven't really gotten the job done, I repeat the whole process. I walk to the front of the church and fill out a response card asking to be baptized. No one thinks this odd. Most of the kids in my youth group have gone up twice to be baptized. A few even go up three times, and one poor soul tried it a fourth but was intercepted by her Sunday school teacher on the way up. We've been so buffaloed by the rules, we are afraid we might be missing one, and when Jesus comes again, we'll be the chaff, not the wheat. Again I step to the back of the pine wall—

this time an old hand at it, not nervous so much as determined. This time I remove my underwear. I know the robe is plenty thick, and when the nice young minister bends me back into the water, no air bubbles form, and the amens are just as loud as they'd been during my earlier, practice baptism. Better safe than sorry, one woman tells me afterward, and I couldn't have agreed more.

In a confusing and conflicting time, I have come to love Jesus as I couldn't love even my mother, and certainly not my brothers. Jesus floods my thoughts and my dreams. He is the one place I can go for a smile, a hug. He is the perfect boyfriend, asking little more than my fidelity. I can immerse myself in Jesus as I'd immersed myself in baptism, and he will be my armor against all the confusion of adolescence, the modernity, the marijuana, the whole sex thing. I will be a good Christian woman, a loaded phrase if ever there was one.

Two

I DON'T WANT
TO PREACH, BUT . . .

Before I begin to date Jesus in earnest, my older brother, at age twelve, gets a call to preach. My middle brother and I are surprised, because there is nothing about him that suggests holiness. He is a precocious child, quick to argue and quick to wrath. He is also the tallest in his class—although he will eventually top out at a lowly five feet ten inches. A good two years before any of his buddies have so much as peach fuzz on their chins, my brother is shaving—not every day, but often enough that we worry.

He is bucktoothed and hairy, with the added disadvantage of perching atop congenitally bowed legs. But he has the good sense to have his teeth knocked out in a childhood accident, and the two fake front teeth the dentist builds him don't protrude nearly as much as do the real ones possessed by me and my middle brother.

Rather than risk ridicule, he makes fun of himself before anyone else can, and early on christens himself "Bo." We'd been taught not to notice defects in people, and so I refuse to use it. I so much want a normal brother who adores me. I want a brother who will beat up boys who tease me for my own buckteeth and hairy legs and bad home haircuts. I want a brother who will play catch with me, and not just when absolutely everyone else on the block is AWOL. I want a brother who will read the books I read and discuss them with me. I don't want a brother who preaches.

But this is selfish and I know it. My brother has problems of his own. He is a magnet for all the condemnation in the house, which is ironic because out in the world, he is beloved. People who aren't related to him by blood or marriage are actually drawn to him. He can work a room, even as a small boy, making people feel they are the most important thing in the world. I don't know how he does this, and I am more than a little jealous of him. People tell the rest of us that they expect great things of him, and his braving that long climb up the stairs to the pulpit lets us all know that he is headed for higher ground.

Up in front of the church—a lofty place I am scared to explore even after services—my brother can barely see over the pulpit. And his voice cracks. But no one laughs, so I don't dare to. My brother is a preacher, albeit of amateur status. My church has an ordination process, although I do not know the exact steps and am not sure who to ask to learn them. We have our own school for preachers down in Louisiana, but all a male of any age must do to start the process is stand in front of the rest of us, mumble a few Scriptures, tell us an anecdote, give us some hope, scare us a little, and they are considered well on their way. Granted, our preachers wear no special title—not "pastor" and certainly not "reverend"—but it is a position set apart from, say, elder or deacon. There is no condemnation if a man doesn't get up to preach, but there is a special mantle that descends upon the shoulders of those who do.

And at twelve!

I should be proud of him, but I'm not. I don't much like him. Outside of church, he is prickly and quick to point out my faults.

Maybe because he is the oldest (boy) and I am the youngest (girl), we are destined to fight over the last bit of milk, the last piece of bread, the small crumbs of attention we both feel are rightfully ours.

Still, even simmering in my jealous stew, I have to acknowledge that it is an incredible feat to get up in front of an entire congregation, even on a Sunday night (the least attended of the three regularly scheduled services). It almost doesn't matter what he says. There he is, his large polyester tie knotted perfectly, his thick black sports glasses slipping onto his nose as he keeps his head down to read his notes. I do not remember the topic, but I think his sermon lasts three minutes, maybe four. As short as it is and as stiff as he is, even I can see that my older brother is a natural. He becomes more fully himself in the pulpit, kinder, more compassionate, the sort of brother you'd want.

Word spreads and my brother rather quickly is asked to speak at area churches. For a while, I think this will be his career, and that about sickens me. He is already too full of himself—or so I think—and being ordained and sanctioned by God to point out everyone else's faults, while it might be a career tailor-made for him, will make him insufferable at family gatherings. We won't be able to curse or tell dirty jokes, even under our breath. We won't be able to gossip and spread tales. He will be our particular cross to bear, our one true Christian, and he will bring happy gatherings to a grinding halt. All this I can see from my pew.

He builds something of a clientele among churches that are between ministers, or smaller congregations that rely on itinerant ministers because the flock is sick of listening to their own male members yammer on. I know he is paid for this, but I don't know how much. Where once he sat in the living room bugging the rest of us, now he is up in his room polishing his next sermon. People tell my mother she must be proud to have such a wonderful son, such a talented boy.

Jealousy is a sin, straight and simple. I don't want to preach, but one Sunday morning, sick at the thought of having to listen to my brother speak again that evening, I work up my nerve to ask my Bible teacher why a woman can't be a preacher.

It is a small town. My Sunday school teacher—a tall, kind man with the reputation of being something of an intellectual—is a family friend. We are bound by two generations of parents who need a break. Years ago, my mother babysat for his wife when she was a little girl, and now I babysit his children, a boy and a girl blessed to live in a modern split-level home in a new development built over my town's old golf course. I have been in their home, had charge over their offspring. I like my Sunday school teacher. I think he knows his Bible better than most, but he is not pompous, and in class he is willing to go off on tangents as some teachers are not. Tangents don't scare him; it almost seems as if he welcomes the diversion. Later, I will understand why he does not feel entirely bound by our lesson books. Eventually, my Sunday school teacher will leave the church over—or so I'm told—a dispute as to whether his presence is required at Sunday-evening services. I am told the elders chastise him for his nonattendance, and he leaves the church for I-don't-know-where. Whatever ties we enjoyed over two generations are severed by his leave-taking, and we never speak of him again.

But before all of that, on this particular Sunday, I simply want an explanation. My brother is hoarding the attention, and I want to know if I might get some, too. I do not want to get into an argument, I promise. A child does not argue with adults. Everyone knows that. I can buy the flood story and the creation story and Jesus hanging on the cross for our sins, but the logic for this one area—restrictions placed on my gender—eludes me and I cannot wait to advance to the next class to ask a teacher with whom I have less emotional ties. I need to know now.

My teacher answers as best he can. He quotes 1 Corinthians

14:34, that women are to keep silent in the assembly,[1] but I am ready for him. I am a voracious reader of my grandfather's *U.S. News & World Report*s and my mother's *Reader's Digest*s. I have recently read an article about Dale Evans, Roy Rogers's wife, in which she said she'd struggled with that verse, since she is a female preacher given to speaking in the assembly. And she said that a biblical scholar—she does not give a name—informed her that in the original language, that verse simply was meant as an admonishment to women who were chatting during church, just like my friends Sherry and Cindy and I do when we think we can get away with it. It is in no way meant to keep women from serving as ministers.

When I tell my teacher this, his already thin lips disappear.

And besides, I say, a literalist to the core, women don't keep silent in the assembly now and nothing bad happens. They chat among themselves, albeit quietly. They pass notes. They hush their babies. That's speaking out in the assembly, isn't it?

He takes a breath and tries again. He cites past precedent. We've never had a woman minister, now, have we? And none of the apostles were women. And Jesus was certainly a man.

Something about the way he says all this makes me think he doesn't quite believe it. It is the tone, his stooped shoulders. What if, I think to myself, he has been waiting for this particular diversion?

No, I say, we haven't had one yet, but that doesn't mean we can't. And if none of the named apostles were women, we certainly have evidence of female disciples, like Dorcas, who was kind to the poor.[2]

1. "Let the women keep silent in the churches; for they are not permitted to speak, but let them subject themselves, just as the Law always says."

2. Dorcas of Joppa, mentioned in Acts 9:36–43. The Aramaic form of the Greek Dorcas is Tabitha, which is also the name of the daughter of the witch Samantha on the TV show *Bewitched*. I suspect no goddess worship/devil conspiracy here. I just raise the fact as an interesting piece of trivia.

And besides, I say, if God made Adam and Eve in his own image, why would women assume a secondary post in the worship of him? I say this and more, reciting my part of all the arguments between my brothers and me in the backseat of my mother's car about what a girl can and can't or should and shouldn't do.

And suddenly I realize something significant. My Sunday school teacher is trained in Bible, but I am schooled in rhetoric. Even though I am nervous and my voice is shaking, I can keep countering his arguments with my own, for the rest of the day if necessary. So long as I remain respectful, I have given this enough thought that I have an answer for everything he says. And I am thrilled and scared at the same time—thrilled because I am holding my verbal own with an adult, and scared for precisely the same reason.

My teacher, bless his heart, is patient, but there is the lesson to complete and other students to consider and I know that my question is edging toward impertinence. Finally he excuses himself, briefly leaves the room, and returns with my bewildered mother. She has been in the nursery, avoiding having to sit through boring Bible classes with the adults, which is something I don't understand because who would want to miss a Bible study? My teacher kindly tells her that I had a question, it was answered, and now perhaps I can spend the rest of class time helping her in the nursery. The meaning is not lost on me. For asking questions, I will be placed among babies who slobber and fill their pants. It is a public shaming.

My mother looks from me to my teacher and back to me, and then she reaches for my shoulder and guides me from the quiet class. She closes the classroom door softly behind us.

What does she say to me as we walk across the lobby to the nursery? I don't remember. I do remember scooting next to her in a pew reserved for the mothers of crying children (no fathers ever went into the nursery) and listening to the Sunday school lesson for adults that was being piped into the room. I risk looking up at her once, and I think I detect the smallest of smiles. Or maybe I just need to see a smile, because I take great strength from that. I choose not to ask her reaction. I don't want to spoil it. This woman who taught me how to hold a baseball bat, surely she doesn't believe what my teacher told me about women and preaching. I am both ashamed at being escorted out of my class by my mother and titillated by the possibility that she approves of what I've done.

And so we sit, me with my mother and the babies. For lack of anything else to do—the babies do not interest me—I listen to the piped-in adult Bible study. My mother is right. It is boring. I will no longer blame her for hiding out in the nursery.

I spend the rest of the week thinking about it and I return to class the next session hardly chastened, but wary. You must pick your battles. I have thought this through. I know that preaching looks glamorous on Sunday mornings when all eyes are on you, but I suspect there is a lot of dirty work involved, a lot of holding hands with sick people, a lot of funerals, which I hate because dead people look like wax candles that have lost their wicks. In my mind, my older brother is just playing at preacher, anyway. If he ever took a job like that for real, he'd see that it's really hard.

And so for now, I will fulfill God's highest purpose for me. I will train myself and pay attention when my Sunday school teachers talk about female virtues. I will learn what is expected of me, and I will surpass those expectations. I will be good.

I will be good, but I also want to shine. There must be a way for me to do that. I am a champion baseball player.[3] I can outrun most of the boys in my class, and I can't imagine not carrying that spirit of competition into church. I am angry that anyone would tell me I can't do something because I'm a girl. Occasionally my brother the preacher reminds me that the most I can hope for is to marry someone in the church, and maybe teach Sunday school to young children. That teasing typically ends with me popping him one,

3. Voted Most Valuable Player in the Webb City Girls Softball League.

and unlike my other brother, the gentle middle child, my older brother, the preacher, the budding man of God, feels no compunction against hitting back. A preacher, my ass.

If my older brother has cornered the market on preaching, and I am the resident rebel, my middle brother is our family musician. He teaches himself to play a host of instruments. I balk when my mother insists I take piano lessons, and so the lessons fall to my middle brother. He flourishes, and the sound of him accompanying his own clear Irish tenor on the old upright fills our house. Sometimes he asks me to harmonize with him. He does this to be kind. The nicest thing he can say about my singing without telling a lie is that I have good rhythm—not a huge factor in the old hymns we sing, but I appreciate his generosity. We discuss it among ourselves and decide he should refrain from playing church songs on the piano or the guitar or any other instrument. Even outside worship, instruments are meant for secular music—or so we conclude.[4] This is a decision we make independent of our parents. Having been steeped in a culture of rules, when lacking them we make up our own.

His success spurs me on.

I want so badly to offer up something to God. I want a talent I can use in worship, but preaching and singing are closed to me, and I suspect being a religious rebel will get me nowhere.

So I throw myself into biblical scholarship. Because I have been so greatly rewarded in school for my ability to memorize, I am sure the same will hold true in Sunday school. So begins my memorization of vast swatches of the Bible—Old and New Testament. I can recite the books and the apostles and the Beatitudes.

4. There are, in fact, no New Testament verses that prohibit instrumental music in church, although there are numerous mentions in the Hebrew Scriptures of instruments and dancing. Augustine said in 354 CE that musical instruments "associate so intimately with the sensual heathen cults, as well as with the wild revelries and shameless performances of the degenerate theater and circus" that the prejudice against them is understandable.

Verses come to me unbidden in quiet moments. I puff up one day when I overhear one of my Sunday school teachers tell another, "That girl knows her Bible."

For most fundamentalists, revelations in the form of spiritual gifts such as speaking in tongues and prophesying are thought to have ended even before the Bible was completely written. Our only line of communication with God is through the Bible. I am taught to keep the line of communication open and to guard that line fiercely. This contributes to what those unfamiliar with the faith consider the fundamentalist's slavish devotion to the Scriptures, to the exclusion of everything else. My friends and I carry our Bibles in specially made little satchels—lacy ones for girls, canvas for boys. We sprinkle our speech with snatches of verses. We are teenage Talmudic scholars in the way we split hairs over Bible passages. We are taught to break down even simple verses like the seemingly straightforward John 3:16—"For God so loved the world that he gave his only begotten Son, that whosoever believes in him should not perish, but have eternal life." That's "should," said our teacher, not "shall." In other words, whoever believes in Jesus might go to heaven, but one couldn't be sure until those pearly gates clang shut behind him or her. We don't have the assurance of the Baptists, who are saved and set for both this life and the next one. We must be on constant guard against the wayward word, the naughty thought that will put us on the wrong side of those gates.

I speak metaphorically. My friends and I know that those pearly gates are a modern-day construct (as is the notion that it will be Peter guarding them).[5] We know that heaven contains no

5. In fact, pearly gates are mentioned in Revelation (21:21), a book we mostly gave over to the Pentecostals, as it made no sense to us. And the verse mentions twelve gates, each gate made of a single pearl. Only later did I realize I could ease up on the people who lived during Jesus's time and didn't accept the way of life he offered. If his prophecies were as obtuse as Revelation, well, perhaps Jesus's contemporaries could be forgiven their skepticism and/or lack of understanding.

such gates, but is a large tract of land filled with just enough mansions for the elect—those favored enough by grace to have been allowed inside. The streets are paved with gold, and while I have a hard time picturing precisely what that looks like, I understand that my only job in heaven is to walk those streets and sing praises to God.[6]

In more honest moments, I can admit that singing for eternity sounds boring to the extreme, but I never say that out loud. In my heart, I prefer the view of heaven handed to me by a Bible-camp counselor. She answered, when asked what we would do throughout our eternity in heaven, "Anything you want." That beats sitting around harmonizing on some old groaner.[7]

Although we are year-round church members, I remember mostly the summers, when I sit in countless Bible classrooms air-conditioned enough to store meat in. Had air-conditioning not been invented, I wonder now how often my family, who could only afford one wall unit that barely cooled our living room, would have darkened a sticky church pew.

Biblical scholarship is encouraged in Sunday-morning and Wednesday-evening Bible class, divided by age and—past a certain age—by gender as well.[8] (And just as we girls wonder what boys' bathrooms looked like, we wonder what goes on in the young men's training classes, other than their practicing their

---

6. The mansion reference most likely comes from John 14:2–3, where Jesus assures his believers that he is leaving to prepare a place for them. The golden streets comes again from Revelation (again 21:21), where the gold is described as looking like transparent glass.

7. But it is, sadly, probably not scriptural.

8. "But I say to you, that everyone who looks on a woman to lust for her has committed adultery with her already in his heart" (Matt. 5:28). Followed by: "And if your right eye makes you stumble, tear it out, and throw it from you; for it is better for you that one of the parts of your body perish, than for your whole body to be thrown into hell" (Matt. 5:29). Oddly, the former verse is taken literally, but incidents of eye plucking, etc., are scant if not nonexistent in my church.

four-minute sermons.) For those of us who want to go, the church also sponsors a week at Green Valley, a small camp outside of Rogers, Arkansas, a ninety-minute drive from our house into the Ozark Mountains of Arkansas, the mythical land of my mother's people, the only mountain range to run east to west (and give birth to people who don't quite fit the mold, either[9]). There, we sleep in moldy cabins on rickety metal bunk beds covered by thin mattresses, attend two Bible classes a day, and practice against one another for the coveted Bible Bowl championship. One year, I spend my free time memorizing our lessons and the Bible verses contained therein, and on the appointed night, I beat my preacher-brother's team single-handedly, because I am the team captain and I hold the buzzer, and I press that thing for all it is worth, answering quietly and calmly while my brother smiles at me from his side of the stage. He is gracious about losing, something I hadn't expected.[10]

I can't wait for Bible camp every year. My parents, I know, look at our week away as a much-needed respite. I look at it as a magical time to swat mosquitoes and not comb my hair and learn more Bible and make friends to whom I will write through the year until the next session. It is a rigorous training ground for future Christians—and many of us are called to baptism in the spring-fed swimming pool. At that pool, afternoon play sessions are divided by gender, an hour for the boys, followed by an hour for the girls.[11] No one seems to realize that if you stand just to the right of the camp store near the worship pavilion, you can see boys in their swim trunks (or girls in their swimsuits) when they climb the ladder to the pool slide.[12] Even today, the rules seem

9. This may appear to be a gratuitous slam against hillbillies. In fact, it is not. I say it with pride.

10. This should not be misconstrued as gratuitous, either. In fact, despite our rocky start, I now love my older brother, for his strength and his courage.

11. Back to Matthew 5:28.

12. "The heart wants what it wants" (Woody Allen, *Time* interview, August 31, 1992).

onerous. The camp website includes this directive: "Bring play clothes (no tank tops, low cut garments, see-through tops, or bare midriffs), swim suit, and dress clothes for evening worship services. Remember, all clothing must be to the top of the knee."[13]

Even in the days of miniskirts, when our youth meetings include the burning of an acrid material we are told is precisely the scent of *mary-jew-anna,* we never question the rules. (And if you are somewhere and you smell that mary-jew-anna, you are to pick up your purse and leave immediately, the same as you would if you thought you smelled gas in the house. Boys who smoke mary-jew-anna will take advantage of you.)

But I love the chill air of the morning, and the smiles of the teachers, and the smell of the woods. On Thursday nights, when we troop up a hill to have a devotion under the stars on the softball field, I believe I can hear God talking.

My proto-feminist discussion with my Sunday school teacher being a notable exception, we do not ask follow-up questions because the answers we get from the first questions we ask are understood to be final. Still. A fundamentalist is a born skeptic. A mention of a Scripture from the pulpit is met by the tissue-hiss of parchment pages as we all frantically turn to the place in the Bible to make sure the speaker is correctly quoting the Word. We are rewarded in Sunday school for knowing our verses, the books of the Bible, the twelve tribes, the twelve apostles, the ten plagues, and the Beatitudes, the most literary part of Jesus's rather rambling Sermon on the Mount.[14] Years later, I tell nonchurched adult friends about the rigorous Bible games we played, and they are horrified. They do not buy my explanation that knowing the Bible was just another way to be considered accomplished so long as you had a talent for memorization. The cadence of the King James Version

13. www.greenvalleybiblecamp.com.
14. "Rambling" may seem harsh, but the sermon does tend to meander.

(the first version I owned) informs the way I think, though I eventually settle on the New International Version, and, finally, the *Ryrie Study Bible,* New American Standard Version. Still, the archaic language of the KJV, while sometimes dense, is so much more colorful: "The Lord is my Shepherd; I shall not want."[15] I particularly love the power and parallelism of the Old Testament—what I later learn in seminary to call the Hebrew Scriptures—where majestic phrases like "the Lord roars from Zion"[16] are bandied about as if the Lord roaring from Zion is something that regularly happens. Elisha and Elijah and Moses and Miriam teach me everything I need to know about courage and honesty and the importance of letting those things go when God demands of you some subterfuge.

But while I learn vast portions of the Bible by heart, I remember not one single lesson on the context of those verses—who wrote them for whom, and why. And it never occurs to me to ask any of those questions. I am taught that the Scriptures are divinely inspired, and that is enough. Whatever human (male) hand held the quill (or so I assume) made no difference. To question authorship was to question God—never a good idea. And so Paul, whom I would come to deeply dislike, took up his writing instrument and spirit-wrote whatever God told him to.[17] Any questions? No? Good.

The heavy emphasis on the Bible and its stories and teachings and my own need to shine in my family make me scripturally lit-

15. The Psalms, including the well-known Twenty-third, written by King David, are not poems but lyrics. They were written to be sung and, not to harp on the whole instrumental-music thing, if David did write them and sing them, he would have most likely accompanied himself on a harp.

16. This phrase is a quote from Amos 1:2. Amos was a sheep breeder from just south of Jerusalem. His words were not popular, as he sought to call people away from pagans and back to God.

17. I try to give Paul a break, but after reading Garry Wills's wonderful 2006 book *What Paul Meant,* I still don't like him. I'm sorry. I just don't.

erate far beyond my Baptist, Methodist, and certainly my Catholic friends, the latter of whom seem almost proud of their lack of biblical knowledge. Their jokes about their own ignorance make me nervous, even while I appreciate the ease with which they approach God's Word. Or not. They don't seem frightened of it, intimidated by it, or bothered by it in the least. Yet I know they are as capable as I of memorizing vast swatches of information, as I'd heard their Catholic prayers and marveled at how they know when to stand up, sit down, and cross themselves, in addition to reciting passages that sound like they were handed down from on high. I envy them their peace.

I also feel sorry for them. When my Catholic friends who are lackadaisical or worse about their Bibles call their church the "one, true church," I sit silently. If they knew their Bible, they'd know that that title belongs to my church, not theirs. I know they are in for a big surprise come Judgment Day, that mythical, just-around-the-corner moment when graves will crack open and the wheat will be separated from the chaff, the lambs from the goats, the church of Christ from the sinners. My teachers say that we have always been here. Always. *We* are the one, true church, the church that can trace its lineage all the way back to the New Testament. We were started by Jesus in 30 CE, on Pentecost, and there's been no break from it since and therefore no need for restoration or a return to the fundamentals of our faith. We never left them. So they said.

Jesus may not have handed us the keys to the church, but fundamentalism isn't a brand-new phenomenon. You are excused if this is news to you. If you dwell in particular portions of the country —say, the coastal regions—this might surprise you. In fact, historians say we peaked around the time women got the vote, and it's all been downhill from there. You are also excused based on your geography. We tend to favor landlocked areas, particularly in the South and Southwest. We hug the Bible Belt. It's not that

we like playing to type or that the big, wide ocean makes us nervous, but historically, the coast is where the new ideas are first col-
lected, from people who arrive here from other places. Flux lives
on the coasts. Fashion starts in the East and moves west. Spiritual
movements start in the West and move east. And bedrock faith
rests in the middle.[18]

Because each congregation in the faith of my girlhood oper-
ates autonomously, with no central hierarchy, what I write about
here refers specifically to the four-hundred-or-so-member church
where I grew up. The denomination churches of Christ—and
that is how the sect should be referred to, as "churches"—may
teach the same thing, but the nuances of interpretation of those
teachings vary, as with the one-cup controversy. What seems like
a silly thing—the vessel from which one sips during the Lord's
Supper—is the cause of much friction among people who insist
they are beneficiaries of the one, true church. At Green Valley
Bible Camp, I met a one-cupper and hardly knew what to say to
her. And frankly, I wondered why they'd let her in.

My church kept silent on most of the great historic conservative (fundamentalist) versus liberal debates. Members of the
church of Christ also decried modernism, but they rarely did so
publicly. If members of my church were quick to step up when
it came to instrumental music or the proper way to partake of
the Lord's Supper, they were—unlike better-known members
of the fundamentalist clan—wary of politics. The one exception
was my church's sponsoring of an anti–equal rights amendment
rally when I was in high school. I attended, of course—the doors
were open—but I sat with my hands balled into fists. Our local
representative spoke from the pulpit, and I was heartily uncomfortable that we would sponsor or wade into a political discussion.
That one exception to my church's rigorous separation from pol-

18. I find absolutely no study backing me up on this, so if I'm wrong on this point,
I apologize. But I think I'm right.

itics bothered me greatly, and it wasn't just the subject matter. I knew the passage of the ERA would not, as the literature said, mean the end of separate toilets for men and women. But why were we, as Christians, weighing in?

This public silence has a lot to do with the churches' insistence on autonomy. Without a governing body over the scattered congregations, it is difficult to speak as one voice. For all kinds of reasons, one minister crying out in the wilderness is easily overlooked.

In the mid-nineteenth century, when the Civil War was tearing a young country out of its adolescence, mainstream Christianity had lost its relevance for many. Some historians say the war itself had soured people on faith in a just God, and some say that religion simply had not kept up, and that Christianity, in particular, was no longer sufficient for the complexities of the emerging culture.

Into this breach stepped evangelicalism, the forerunner of fundamentalism. And while groups like the Baptists split over the slavery question, given the lack of central organization, the new evangelicals—united in their belief in the Bible as the final authority—remained viable. The 1860 census counts 225,000 in 2,070 congregations. That made them the seventh-largest Christian group in the nation at the time—and the fastest growing.

Here is where things get tricky. We need definitions.

"Evangelical" comes from the Greek word *euangelion,* which means good news, or gospel. Unlike "fundamentalist," which can be used to describe a segment of any religious population, "evangelical" has traditionally been applied to Protestant Christians alone. The word became common in Great Britain and America as applied to a religious movement that swept back and forth across the English-speaking world in the latter parts of the eighteenth and nineteenth centuries. Although the word has fallen out of favor in mainstream culture, fundamentalism "was a loose, diverse, and changing federation of co-belligerents united by their fierce opposition to modernist attempts to bring Christianity into line with modern thought," according to historian George M. Marsden. A coarser definition is this: A fundamentalist is an evangelical who is pissed off about something. The cleaner version of this definition may have originated with the Reverend Jerry Falwell; I'm fairly certain Falwell did not use the word "pissed."

While every fundamentalist is an evangelical, not every evangelical is a fundamentalist. An evangelical can be downright ecumenical—meaning an evangelical can be perfectly accepting of other faiths.

Not so a fundamentalist. In short, a fundamentalist:

- Believes strongly in the inerrancy of the Bible and has little use for a contextual study of it. A more liberal evangelical—say, former president Jimmy Carter—does not cling to the idea of biblical inerrancy.
- Believes that people who aren't fundamentalist aren't really Christian. That is a hard point. To be a true fundamentalist, you must believe that your friends who aren't fundamentalist are going to hell.
- Will not debate religion and sees no purpose in such debate. A popular bumper sticker in my hometown said, "God Said It, I Believe It, That Settles It." A debate means the fundamentalist would be debating for God, and what if the fundamentalist isn't up to it?
- Sees the Holy as entirely masculine—God the Father and Jesus the Son. The sexually ambivalent Holy Spirit is—as you might imagine—considerably far less powerful.
- Believes their church can be traced back to the New Testament. It is the one, true Church. Sorry, Rome.

Perhaps you can see the circular arguments such beliefs can foster. Once, in a junior high English class, I am asked to debate whether marijuana should be legalized. I have not yet embraced the notion that religion is not something to be debated. In fact, I believe we all agree on its importance. Therefore, there is no *need* for debate. (A small but crucial distinction.) When the time comes, I stand up and read 1 Corinthians 6:19–20: "Or do you not know that your body is a temple of the Holy Spirit, who is in you, whom you have from God, and that you are not your own? For you have been bought with a price: therefore glorify God in your body." When I finish the Scripture, I sit back down again, entirely satisfied with my logic. I can't imagine what my debating opponent thought, and to me it didn't much matter.

In fact, I am from the Stone-Campbell (the latter is of small relation, not enough to earn me a seat in heaven) movement, a group of believers who embraced the teachings of Alexander Campbell, a theologian who lived in the 1800s and who, with his father, Thomas, helped bring on the Restoration Movement in American religion. With people like Kentucky minister Barton Stone (the Stone in the movement's name), the men staged fervent camp meetings meant to unite Christians under one tent. Thomas Campbell initiated the creed, "Where the Bible speaks, we speak, and where the Bible is silent, we are silent." I heard that phrase growing up, though I learned of its author only later. He also said that the New Testament was "a perfect constitution for the worship, discipline, and government of the New Testament Church, and as perfect a rule for the particular duties of its members."[19]

Some factions interpreted Thomas Campbell's writings to mean that ecumenicalism was the answer, the "can't we all just get along" school of thinking. Mine didn't. Mine thought Campbell meant to remove what they saw as the latter-day additions to the religious workings and return to a true New Testament faith, ecumenicalism be damned.

19. Upon first glance, the Campbells seem a little scary in their dourness. But their message isn't dour. There is some real hope and glory in what they are calling for. You just have to look for it.

Again, I will learn this only later, after leaving both Missouri and the church of my youth, when I enroll in Hartford Seminary, in Connecticut. Growing up, my part of Christendom didn't acknowledge their connection to the Stone-Campbell movement or the Restoration Movement or the Enlightenment or any notion that religion evolves over time.[20] Nor did I then draw the connection between us and the Puritans, another form of fundamentalism, although the Puritans wouldn't have identified themselves as such, either. The Puritans' Bible was their literal guide, and those not subscribing to that belief were judged to be in danger of hellfire. The sect—or group, or cult—chose to isolate itself from the rest of the world, for fear of contamination by more modern beliefs. Puritans saw themselves as the holders of the keys to the kingdom. They and they alone had stripped away the folderol that had accumulated over the centuries, to reveal a pure and true faith.

If most modern-day fundamentalists would not have identified with the Puritans, their own approach to God began to take shape in the early part of the twentieth century, when two California businessmen decided that the world had veered too far off its fundamental axis. The men, brothers Milton and Lyman Stewart, grew up in Pennsylvania, the sons of a tanner. Lyman Stewart longed to be a missionary, but he went broke as a result of a bad oil investment. (He would later go on to found the highly successful Union Oil Company.) Lyman Stewart was so pious that the site of his California business came to be known as Christian Hill—and that probably was not a compliment. The brothers decided that modernism was eating away at the fiber of the culture. At the time, modernism included everything from woman suffrage to dances to movie theaters. The Stewarts decided to hold the line by printing three million copies of a twelve-volume tract known

20. Jesus Christ is the same yesterday and today, yes and forever (Heb. 13:8). And so should be his church—or so we believed.

as *The Fundamentals: A Testimony to the Truth*. It began: "In 1909 God moved two Christian laymen to set aside a large sum of money for issuing twelve volumes that would set forth the fundamentals of the Christian faith, and which were to be sent free of charge to ministers of the gospel, missionaries, Sunday school superintendents, and others engaged in aggressive Christian work throughout the English speaking world." The fundamentals included belief in the inerrancy of Scripture, the deity of Christ, atonement, Christ's resurrection from the dead, and his return at the Second Coming.

According to Marsden, a copy is indeed supposed to have been sent to "every pastor, missionary, theological professor, theological student, YMCA and YWCA secretary, college professor, Sunday school superintendent, and religious editor in the English-speaking world." In the days before television and the Internet, the Stewarts figured out how to most effectively spread the word.

Their decision to reach back to what they imagined was the authentic core of Christianity was understandable, considering the social and cultural tumult of their times. Race riots, riots against immigrants, strikes, and other upheavals were ripping the country apart. The Cross is an anchor in troubled times, so the Stewarts went back to the Campbells and their "primitive" Christianity. What is it that fundamentalism offers better than just about any other social salve? A definite yes or no when you're not comfortable with the maybes.

The World Christian Fundamentals Association met in 1919 in Philadelphia.[21] The next year, William Jennings Bryan, three-time unsuccessful candidate for U.S. president, took up the banner and became the movement's most recognized spokesman.

---

21. The conference was organized by Kentucky-born Baptist minister William B. Riley, who combined an austere approach to the Scriptures and a dogged devotion to an activist church. Six thousand believers listened to Riley decry modernism and call for greater church involvement in politics and society.

John Roach Straton—who later would lead the charge against presidential candidate (and Roman Catholic) Al Smith—became known—ironically—as the Pope of Fundamentalism. In 1925 Bryan would win the famed Scopes Monkey Trial (the teacher in question, John Thomas Scopes, was convicted and charged a one-hundred-dollar fine for teaching evolution in defiance of Tennessee law), but Scopes's attorney, Clarence Darrow, was far more impressive, in part by showing that Bryan didn't know nearly as much Bible as any committed fundamentalist is supposed to. After the trial, the students at Dayton High, where Scopes taught, threw Darrow a dance. A week later, Bryan dropped dead after eating a big plate of fried chicken. And then the Tennessee Supreme Court reversed the lower court's decision. It was, for all practical purposes, the death knell of fundamentalism, and it was only 1926. For years, Prohibition was considered fundamentalism's last gasp with respect to national politics.

The backlash against the Stewarts' vision of paradise was swift. Influential newspaper columnist H. L. Mencken made a career of painting the fundamentalist as a rube. His bon mots include:

> "The trouble with Communism is the Communists, just as the trouble with Christianity is the Christians."

> "The Christian church, in its attitude toward science, shows the mind of a more or less enlightened man of the Thirteenth Century. It no longer believes that the earth is flat, but it is still convinced that prayer can cure after medicine fails."

> Puritanism is "the haunting fear that someone, somewhere, may be happy."

> The fundamentalist "is quite unable to grasp the complex evidences upon which the civilized minority bases its heresies, and so he seeks refuge in the sublime simplicities of revelation."

You can see he had an ax to grind, and grind it he did, most eloquently.

The fundamentalists' ability to fight back against public opinion was hampered greatly by their lack of hierarchy, which would have given them spokespeople—most likely spokesmen. Without a core leadership, fundamentalists couldn't agree on issues as important as slavery and as tangential (to most) as the use of instrumental music in the worship. But any religion quickly becomes a denomination, and the more conservative group, whose members called themselves the churches of Christ, split off in the early 1900s. It was, to put it bluntly, frontier revivalism frozen in amber. And so it remains.

If that sounds grim, it isn't. If it sounds soulless, it isn't that, either. The traditions plant in the believer—even someone who walks away from the church—a deep and soulful need.

Three

KNOCKING DOORS FOR JESUS

I am standing at a chain-link fence that feels like thin protection against the snarling dog on the other side, and I am frightened, and if the dog could speak, I believe it would say, "You are a lousy Christian."[1]

I don't know the breed, but if I had to guess I would say German shepherd. Most of my neighbors have the same dog, broad of chest, large of head, expert at snarling and growling and protecting their owners' meager belongings from would-be burglars or conniving ex-wives. For a while, we had the same dog, or one very much like it. We kept him tied to an unpainted doghouse out back, and rather than walking him as I now would know to do, we rotated the responsibility of helping get Tinker untangled from his self-tied Gordian knots. On the few times he broke loose he let everyone know about his dissatisfaction with a short rope by jumping on neighborhood children. That's all he did, jump, but he was a big dog and it was scary and he finally jumped on one

---

1. Don't laugh. A German study released in 2004 said that a border collie had mastered two hundred words.

too many, and then we didn't have him anymore. My stepfather says that he took Tinker to live on a farm, a mythical place where the owners love troublesome animals and there is plenty of room for Tinker to run off his excess energy. I would hear about this farm—always just over the horizon, and no, we can't visit, sorry —my entire girlhood. This wonderful place was the repository for all of our pets who went wrong—namely, all of our pets. Later, my brother the preacher—who also removed from me the belief in Santa and the Easter Bunny—told me there was no such farm, that our stepfather had simply taken Tinker and the other disappeared animals and left them on a country road somewhere.

I couldn't have told you Tinker's exact breed, either, but I knew the type. And I knew better than to try something stupid, like say, "Nice doggie," and open the gate.

I am a soldier for the Lord, dressed in a scratchy slip and my Sunday shoes, and if these were Old Testament times the rose of Sharon bush by the front door would burst into flames or something.[2] But we are in the final days, and even though those times are scarier than any before them, I carry only a notebook and a folded pink sheet tucked inside my Bible (my sword). The sheet contains the first segment in my church's series of Bible lessons, called Open Bible Study, which we refer to as OBS. (That the acronym might be understood as "Oh, BS!" is lost on us. If someone, a more worldly someone, had pointed it out to us, I'm sure we would have changed it, but no one did and so we remained blissfully unaware of how coarser types might view what we were peddling.)

My purpose is to get inside the gate, and then inside the house, and convince the sinner living in error there that he (or she) needs to sit with me for four separate lessons of OBS, the questions of which will gently but insistently lead him (or her) to the Lord. It must be said that even without me sitting there walking the sin-

2. There's precedent: Exodus 3:2–4.

ner through the lessons, the questions are pretty easy. They ask things like, "Do you want to spend eternity in hellfire?" We have been told that anyone who would answer yes to that is probably retarded and so if that happens, we are to politely dismiss ourselves and leave, because God always lets retarded people into heaven for free, just as he lets in children.[3] Better to expend your energies on the tougher sells, like Catholics.

It is never discussed—at least not out loud—but I have a sense that the souls of the members of various denominations are somehow weighted. The closer the denomination's theology is to our own, the less points one earns for effecting a conversion. Members of the denominations that are more far afield are worth more. I am speaking cosmically, of course. There is no scorecard that we can see—but God sees all and records all and I get the sense that he particularly likes it when we bring in someone whose theology is nowhere near right. I can find no Scriptures to back this up, but anecdotally, if we get a new member and that person has been raised a Roman Catholic, that person is accorded a special place in the service. It is as if we must reward the person—and the Christian who brought them to the True Way—for their relatively longer journey. Bagging a Methodist would be nice, but a Roman Catholic—or a Jew, if we could find one!—is even better. Methodists do err in their use of instrumental music, but their overall services resemble our own. But with Catholics' bells and smells and standing up and sitting down and rote memorization of manmade words? Now that's a soul![4]

I secretly harbor the hope that every house contains a Catholic who wants a simpler way where they don't have to pray through an intercessory, one of those obscure saints. My best friend, Alan, is a Roman Catholic, and while I have made only halfhearted efforts at converting him, I later sneak out of the house to attend

---

3. There's precedent for this, too: Matthew 19:14.
4. This, I'm pretty sure, is not at all scripturally based.

Midnight Mass with him. The incense and the music are over-whelming, even if I understand perhaps a fifth of what is go-ing on. Of course, the best thing would be if I could bring him to Christ, and then we could get married, but that doesn't look to be a possibility. Alan likes cute and perky cheerleaders. And he seems happy to be a Catholic. And I know his conversion would kill his mother, a big, laughing Italian woman who makes won-derful pasta from scratch, and so, given the potential fallout, I don't push it.

I stick with seeking to harvest the souls of strangers, the peo-ple I don't know. This should be easy, I think, as I clutch my Bible, listen to the maniacal dog condemn me as it flings itself into the gate, and ponder my options.

I could walk away, but I am not wired to do that.[5] On the other side of the dog is a hopeless and helpless sinner. One of the tenets of an evangelical's faith is to share the gospel.[6] It's not an option to bow out. Because sharing my faith is so important, I will overcome my innate shyness to knock doors for Jesus.[7] I am fourteen in my memory, but I started at age twelve—which from this distance probably sounds a little like child abuse. What right-thinking parents send daughters out into the world to knock on the doors of strangers, even if it is to try to win souls for Jesus?

In my case, my parents had nothing to do with it. My parents never knocked doors themselves and never pushed my evangeliz-ing; it was as if they'd introduced us to something that merely caught their attention but absolutely consumed my brothers and

5. Much was made in my Sunday school classes about putting on the whole ar-mor of God mentioned in Ephesians 6:11–13. Someone who is fully armored isn't going to let a little thing like a mad dog deter her.

6. In fact, in addition to our armor, much was made of what we called our Great Commission, most notably recorded in Matthew 28:18–20, that we go into all the world to preach the gospel to every creature.

7. The proper phrase is "knock on doors for Jesus," but maybe because we do it and talk about it so much, we shorten it to "knock doors."

myself. I knocked doors of my own accord, because I wanted to be a good Christian, and good Christians are not afraid to go into the highways and byways to find souls for Christ. Look at the early disciples. Look specifically at the martyred ones.[8] They walked bravely into the world and didn't care for their own lives, much less whether they looked dorky knocking on doors or lintels or whatever they knocked back then. In weaker moments, I remind myself that the early Christians could always whip up a little miracle here and there, which at least would have drawn a crowd. I can't even tell a good joke. Given that the bush won't burst into flames, and given that I can't strike a tree dead—or, better yet, turn water into wine—I must rely on something less obvious to get me inside the gate.

But, boy! Would I like to perform a miracle. Maybe I could just kill the dog with a thunderbolt. I know that I am mixing deities here; it was Zeus who held the thunderbolt. But at this point help from any corner would be appreciated.

Killing a dog—even with something as sexy as a thunderbolt —is unkind and I know it and I hate this about myself, the random, violent thought that will, like a chain I'm building, drag me down to hell. I often think of acquiring special powers that enable me to chop down an adversary with a thunderbolt or inflict him (or her) with blindness, and I know that is a bad thing, because as you think, so you do. They say that all the time in Sunday school, and even though I have no way of actually striking a mad dog dead with a thunderbolt, thinking it is the same as doing it. We are told you cannot think lustful thoughts. Well, you can, but you shouldn't. While the rest of the country snickered at then presidential candidate Jimmy Carter's assertion (in *Playboy* magazine, no less) that he had committed sin because he'd lusted for a

---

8. In this, the Catholics had it all over us. The actual Scriptures are vague on the torture and murder of early Christians, unlike Catholic teachings, where the details of the deaths of numerous recorded martyrs are PG-13, if not R rated.

woman in his heart, people of my particular religious stripe nod-
ded our heads in recognition.[9] Yes, Lord. So if Jimmy's noticing a
pretty girl counted, certainly thinking about killing a dog is taboo.
I stand here armed with the sword of the Lord, but in truth, I am
afraid. Say I get past the dog. That's only the half of it. You never
know what is beyond the door. It might be a drunk. It might be
someone who works nights and doesn't appreciate being awak-
ened by a Bible thumper, even a well-meaning one. They might
be angry or worse.

My faith is shaky and I know it. My survival instinct often
gets in the way of living a good life. Instead of trusting God to take
care of me, I am a gutless wonder standing on the wrong side of
the gate—the soulless side—telling myself that the dog might
be mad, rabid. The adults in my life use the threat of rabid dogs
(and drunken men) to rule my childhood. My grandmother will
run out and snatch us bald-headed[10] if we stay in the yard when
there's a stray dog around, especially one that walks funny. I don't
remember ever actually seeing a rabid dog, but the rumors are
enough to keep us on guard. We are on constant watch for a dog
gone mad, or a strange man walking through the neighborhood.
Never mind that the drunk men who come to our door are hoboes
and that my grandmother always makes them a sandwich after
she secures us children inside in front of the television. She never
makes a big deal out of making those sandwiches and she never
tells my mother—whose food it is—what she does. Meanwhile,
my mother comes home from the shirt factory and marvels at how
fast her children go through a loaf of bread.[11]

If this dog was foaming at the mouth it wouldn't look more

9. I refer again to Matthew 5:28.

10. To "snatch us bald-headed" was akin to "yanking a knot in our tails." We
would be punished, corporeally.

11. I feel fortunate to have met hoboes in my youth. We lived within the mournful sound of a Frisco freight line. The men would shuffle up to the back door, and
my grandmother would look up from her frying chicken and, without a word, make
the men a sandwich.

threatening. Seeing that it can't throw itself through the chain-link, it has now started to spring into the air, trying, I believe, to leap over the fence. With each successive bounce, the dog looks more likely to clear the barrier. And then what? I have scouted the landscape and I see only a small, spindly catalpa tree nearby. It might not hold my weight, and it certainly won't hold mine and Sherry's, my partner for door knocking today. And then I remember a sermon Brother Webb preached once, which started with an anecdote of two men stumbling onto a bear. They take off running and one man pulls ahead; the other man, the one falling behind, cries out that they'll never outrun the bear, and the man in front says, "I don't have to outrun the bear, I just have to outrun you!" That got a big laugh. I don't know the scriptural message that followed, but I liked the joke and I cling to the message. I don't have to outrun the dog. I just have to outrun Sherry. But, like contemplating killing the dog, that's not very Christian of me, is it? Still, I got the idea from a sermon, and most sermons are—are they not?—scripturally based.

Surely it won't come to that, me outrunning my friend and fellow door-knocker. Surely God will watch over us as we do what is, after all, his work. Failing that, surely the dog's owner will hear the ruckus. Surely he or she will come out soon, collar the beast, and let me inside.

"You leave that dog alone!" a neighbor calls out, and when I yell over and explain that we're not bothering the dog, the old woman goes inside and slams the door behind her. Fine. Now I know what kind of reception we'll get next door and at least that bit of uncertainty is eliminated from my day.

Maybe this dog has been trained specially to smell the ink in a Bible and guard against people like me. We have been told to ignore the signs on doors that say "No Solicitors," as "solicit" means to sell, and the word of God is free.[12] This is a fine point often lost

12. "For the wages of sin is death, but the free gift of God is eternal life in Christ Jesus our Lord" (Rom. 6:23).

on the dwellers of the houses we visit, and I have had my fill of explaining that we're not technically selling anything, simply sharing it freely.[13]

Usually, my friends Sherry and Cindy and I trade off as each other's partner in this useless endeavor. In all the years I knock doors (roughly ten of them, although I am much more dedicated in my teen years than in my twenties), I convince only one sad man in a dirty T-shirt to sign up for OBS. And he quits after the first pink sheet, never advancing to the green, the blue, or the all-important yellow. I know that true Bible students don't rely on the crutch of OBS, because they know precisely the Scriptures to use to convince a sinner. I know Scriptures, but I don't trust myself in the clinch to remember the right ones. The OBS is supposed to render conversion easy. The sinner says yes to an in-home study, and then I and a church elder sit down with said sinner and together we fill out the forms until on the last page the sinner cries out, "I am a sinner!" and asks to be baptized. And, boom, there would go a sinner's pelt on my belt and I would be among the holy, no doubt about it.[14]

Truth to tell, though, I know of no one from my youth group who has successfully snagged a sinner by means of OBS. And if one does, it most likely won't be me. For one, I am unable to overcome the hurdle of a snarling dog. For two, even if I were in-

---

13. Sharing among fundamentalists should know no bounds. We are taught that our Jewish fore-families tithed, or gave a tenth—with some substitutions possible. We are taught that tithing is for weenies, with the example in Mark 12:42 of the poor widow and her copper coins—giving a penny that was implied to be worth far more than the money given by anyone else who'd contributed.

14. Precisely what happened when a soul was saved was a little sketchy to me. The name of the blessed could obviously not be recorded until Judgment Day, and so even though the angels rejoiced when someone was brought to the Lord, they only rejoiced for a while, given that the blessed could certainly sin and lose his or her holy status.

side the gate, I don't have the heart to convince most people that their lives are in error—living, as I do, in complete uncertainty about my own. Frankly, it seems rude to intrude upon their lives and rain down hellfire when all people want to do on a regular Saturday morning is get out the door to go to the Piggly Wiggly or enjoy some peace and quiet while their children watch Saturday-morning cartoons. I have enough fire to knock the door, but not enough to make the sale. So I usually don't push it. When I finally do get one of them on the stoop, I nearly stand on my head to feed them answers that will save us both a lot of time and trouble (and disappointment). And even though my soul and yours depends on this, I sometimes even lie on the little form I'm supposed to fill out that lists every address on any given street. I write by them NOAH, for No One At Home, which I have no way of knowing because I don't even try the doors. When I chance upon someone, I usually just talk to them a bit and ask them to come to church sometime, and while most of them are polite and say things like, "Well, I just may," we both know that is hillbilly code for "No, thank you."[15] We also know that if we try to puncture that courtesy's thin skin, we both will regret it. Feelings will be hurt, so I choose not to push it, even though my minister and my youth minister tell me that my soul's own fate is hanging on this, on my ability to reach the lost. But I only fake a NOAH when I go out by myself. If I have a partner, I can't very well lie, can I?

I feel like a creep about this. There are kids in my youth group who, even though they bring not one solitary soul to Jesus, seem to thrive on this, the thrill of the hunt. I do not understand what is wrong with me. I love Jesus and I want to bring souls to him. And here we are, giving up half our Saturdays and going out

15. One day, when I am very old, I will write a book and name it *The Way of the Hillbilly,* in order to preserve the niceties of the culture and not just the goofy parts.

every week, every single week no matter the weather, to try to get someone—anyone—to come to Jesus. That's a hymn we sing, "Come to Jesus, He will save you, though your sins as crimson glow," a line that always catches in my net. I could sing the rest of the song ("If you give your heart to Jesus, He will make it white as snow...") but my mind snags on that one image, that our sins follow us around, written out in script in neon-red lights. I worry about what my own neon says, but when I talk to these sad people, I don't see any red. I see abject poverty and houses that smell like last week's dinners and windows painted shut and children in clothes that hang off their thin shoulders. These are my neighbors and I know they're struggling, with overdue rent and cars that don't start, and I haven't the heart to send them to hell on top of all that, figuratively or otherwise. As much as it weighs on my soul, I opt, instead, to let the sinners go free. Perhaps somewhere down the road, if God really loves them, they will find their way to him. This is my prayer.

The dog is still barking, and Sherry has wandered over to the next door, to the woman who slammed the door on us. I figure to give it a few more seconds and then record a NOAH. Even with the marvelous examples set by the martyrs, there's no reason for me to die for my religion—or, more accurately, for the off chance that the owner of this residence will prove to be fertile ground, anything better than a swine before which pearls are about to be strewn.

I *am* a creep about this. I must not love Jesus enough. God fuels my friends, who smile and pound on doors and no matter how many times they are rejected, they keep going. God fuels them, or they would take each rejection personally. I can't do that. I can't convince myself that the woman who sighs and tells me that she already goes to church is in danger of hellfire. I don't have the heart to tell her that she might be going to church, but it's not the right church, and therefore it's not really church at all. I know that's the case, that there is no salvation outside of Jesus—my brand of Jesus, the one we worship at Fourth and Forest church of Christ. But still.

The sad state of my failure as a winner of souls was set early. One weekend when I am nine, my family goes on a rare vacation to Grand Lake O' the Cherokees (spelled just like that). This is during a period when I am at my holiest, when I watch every p and q in my life and others' to see if I know anyone who actually can stay on the straight and narrow. I try to do a good deed every day— and then I amp it up and try to do a good deed and not brag about it.[16] This is my fiercest time for underlining Scriptures, for seeing spiritual meaning in everything.

I don't have hordes of friends, but I don't mind.[17]

On this particular steamy Saturday, as I float on the water in a sticky inner-tube, an older woman named Pat floats over on a tube of her own. We begin chatting, and it turns out that she, too, belongs to a church that means a great deal to her. At first we simply exchange anecdotes about what our respective churches mean to us, but then—gladiators that we are—someone pulls a sword. Someone says something disparaging about the other's belief. (Pat is Pentecostal, and so believes in the gifts of the Spirit like speaking in tongues and the laying on of hands to heal the sick. I am not Pentecostal, and I know that gifts of the Spirit were specifically meant for the early church—kind of like party tricks to draw a crowd—and that that time is over and anyone who thinks differ-

---

16. I drew for my inspiration on a really great rousing hymn with a strong bass part: "A Beautiful Life," that includes the words, "Each day I'll do a golden deed by helping those who are in need. My life on earth is but a span and so I'll do (and so I'll do) the best I can (the best I can)."

17. "Blessed are you when men cast insults at you, and persecute you, and say all kinds of evil against you falsely, on account of me" (Matt. 5:11). In that way, being excluded from the cool kids is a bit of a coup.

ently is in for a huge awakening come Judgment Day, buster.) We begin to argue. I don't see that coming, but passion will do that to you. Pat is the first Pentecostal with whom I've explored theology, and our talking gets pretty heated over healing and speaking in tongues, things that, I try to explain to her, cannot actually happen, sorry. When my parents finally call me to a lakeside meal, the woman and I are in full-bore battle. We are not shouting at each other, but we—I, at least—are barely waiting for the other to finish before we—I—issue a rejoinder. I am surprised that she is not seeing the logic of what I am saying. If she was my age, I most likely would have splashed her, but she is at least as old as my grandmother and therefore immune to physical retaliation. Before I paddle off, we exchange addresses, and as soon as I get home, I fire off a letter, the contents of which I crib from one of our many church tracts. At my church, we are quite enamored of tracts—usually a typewriter sheet folded into threes, containing little cartoon characters running from the devil. They cover everything from premarital sex—a big no—to not putting enough money in the collection plate—not as bad as premarital sex, but pretty bad.

We keep our tracts on a large display board near the front door of the church, and I always have a few at home, just for reference. They are free. I grab a handful whenever a new one arrives. It is our version of *The Fundamentals,* our beliefs laid out in simple, portable form. It is a quick way to define my religion —and a powerful tool to use against people like my new lakeside friend. You never know when you might have an opportunity to teach someone—even if you are an insufferable nine-year-old floating in a baggy swimsuit on a sticky inner-tube. The Lord works in mysterious ways.

Pat and I write back and forth three or four times until I begin to tire of spending pretty summer days at my mother's hand-me-down typewriter, transcribing the latest pertinent tract for my new friend. I suppose I could just slip a tract in the mail to her, but that would prove to her, in my nine-year-old mind, that I am relying on other sources and not my own impressive Bible knowledge.[18] I don't know who stops writing first, but I bet it is me. I'm a kid, after all.

And so even cribbing from the writing of the really smart people who compose our tracts, I can't bring a soul to Christ.

Later, in high school, I bomb as a missionary too. A young couple I adore in our church sign up to go to Papua New Guinea, to teach the dark people the ways of the Lord. The woman has been raised in the church, and her father is my favorite elder there. He is tall and his hands are the size of laundry baskets. He loves his tiny wife—a feminine woman named Bonnie whose hair, even at church camp, is never less than lacquered—and I love them as if they were my own family. The missionary man came to the church later in life, like in his twenties, through his wife. I hear that before he'd been baptized he'd been a bit of a bad boy. That, of course, makes him doubly attractive to me in a way I can't explain then or now. Jesus had come into his heart and changed him for the better, even elevated him above the rest of us everyday Christians to be a missionary. That impressed me a great deal. I considered myself a garden-variety Christian, and what the missionary couple are doing is interesting to the extreme.

They come home with fantastic stories and beautiful wood carvings, and I show too much interest because before long they are talking to me about being a missionary with them. They say I can fly back with them to the island, which I look up on a map. It is far, far away. I would live among people who pinched their lips with bones and I would bring them to Jesus. Maybe, I think, I would do better in a foreign land. Maybe if I had to learn another language, I would learn the language of salvation as well. Rich people are entirely too settled, too happy, too well off to care about

18. And here's where I hoisted myself on my own petard. From Proverbs 16:18: "Pride goes before destruction, and a haughty spirit before stumbling."

any gospel message. Everyone knows that poor people make better Christians.[19] Who could be poorer than New Guinea natives who pinch their lips with bones?

On the other hand, I can't bring a sad man in a dirty T-shirt to Jesus. What hope do I have shouting across a language barrier? And what if they have religions they like already, something that doesn't involve church at all but gets them through the days and nights? It is tantamount to heresy, what I am thinking, and I don't want to think like that, so when the time comes to make my decision, I lie. I tell the young couple that I need to stay in school and I thank them for the opportunity. They are nice about it, and I feel sorry for them. I think they see in me something that isn't there and that makes me sad. I cannot afford to admit to myself that the mission system is flawed, that it carries with it more than the whiff of colonialism inflicted on cultures that operate fine without us. At the time, I see my inability to bring souls to Jesus as a failure on my part. I suspect it is lack of faith. And that bothers me more than I can say.

Instead, I indulge in my own form of missionary work. In the '70s and early '80s, churches in the South and Midwest bought old school buses and painted them and used them to pick up children who otherwise would not have been able to get to church. The idea is simple: the churches refurbish old church buses, and volunteers ride through the neighborhoods and convince children to ride the bus to church. Rather than waste time looking out the window, we provide Bible stories and games on the ride—a kind of rolling Sunday school, only more fun. We hand out doughnuts and candy, and that makes us very popular among the poor kids of Joplin, Missouri. Although the idea is that we will win families to Jesus through the children, the parents never accompany their

---

19. "And Jesus said to his disciples, 'Truly I say to you, it is hard for a rich man to enter the kingdom of heaven. And again I say to you, it is easier for a camel to go through the eye of a needle, than for a rich man to enter the kingdom of God'" (Matt. 19:23–24).

children on the bus. They are, however, happy to send them. And so our buses fill with hungry kids who need more than the dough-nuts and hand-me-down clothes we can give them.

As the teacher, I leave for church two hours early to face those happy children and lead them in songs and Bible stories as we complete our hour-long route. In the beginning, it is hard to stand on the moving bus, even with my knees braced against a seat, but I get the hang of it. I make flash cards (on construction paper bought with my babysitting money) of famous biblical charac-ters.[20] We chant Bible verses and play games where the prize is a piece of penny candy. Or a stamped comb. And I stay to take them all home after all three services. I become a surrogate big sister for these children whose parents don't love them enough to take them to church. I am vomited on, pooped on (give the little boy some credit; at least he was mortified), and given hugs by children too dirty to be in church. And then I visit them on Saturday mornings to remind them they are getting a ride. I see homes that smell bad and meet parents who are so beaten down they can barely work up the energy to shake my hand. The goal is to bring the whole family to church, but the parents use the quiet time to sleep, I think. As we knock doors looking for riders, we find an old blind man named Ralph, who calls me Susie. He lives in one of the bro-ken-down hotels on Main Street in Joplin, and he never seems to mind the noise from the children. We help him onboard—he never misses a service—and I am close enough to tell that he does not bathe properly. But I kiss him on the cheek every time I see him. It is expected.

It is the social gospel at work, and I love it.[21] It is social work, with the added bonus of saving sinners' souls. My brother (the

20. An example: draw a picture of a knee (with arrows pointing to it, for clarity), and then a bed, and then a raccoon, and then the letters *EZR,* and you have Neb-uchadnezzar, the Babylonian king.

21. In fact, my church was a part of the social gospel movement, but then we lost interest. More on that later.

singer, not the preacher) drives and I teach and together we build
our route until it has to be split and split again. We hold picnics.
We organize church Olympics.[22] Religion is fun! And we make it
so. We whip the kids into a frenzy and then deliver them, candy-
crazed and tired out, to church. On the way home, we mostly just
sing. Our discipline problems are minor.

We engage in fierce cross-town competition with an Assembly of God church that has purchased an old theater on Main
Street. Their bus ministry is much better financed. We hear rumors that they offered pony rides, helicopter rides, and the like, in
addition to doughnuts and candy. We can't compete. We are shoe-
string. We pay for most everything ourselves. It is unbearable, but
we tell ourselves that we are winning souls to the gospel, not brib-
ing poor kids. "What you win them with, you win them to," we
sniff, and we feel a little better.

We solicit clothes that might fit our riders. That is the fun
part, the part where the pleading is buried. One church member
tells me, "You have to wrap the gospel in a peanut butter sandwich." But then the church elders begin to notice that we are only
attracting children, not adults. Despite our protests—we quote
Jesus, "Suffer the little children to come unto me," Mark 10:14,
of course—the Sunday-night routes are cut, then the Wednesday-
night routes. I think we are being hypocritical. All this time we
have told the children they need to come to church three times
a week, and then we stop giving them rides, just like that. Eventually the elders vote to stop the Sunday-morning routes too. Though
we continue to pick up a few stragglers in our cars, eventually,
with the doughnuts and games and candy gone, they fall away.

No one says so, but the bus ministry mirrors the early days
of my church—and the vote to disband the bus ministry is a

---

22. We are fidgety, my family. When we gather, we talk better if we toss a football or a baseball back and forth. We assume the same is true for everyone.

smaller version of what happened earlier, as well. Despite fundamentalism's original role as a social and political force, a strict adherence to the idea of right versus wrong got in the way. At the movement's beginning, its adherents came from lower- and middle-class families, agrarians, artisans, and small entrepreneurial families most adversely affected by urban and individual change. The rest of the world, in fact, was seen as a threat to the family, as a harbinger of deterioration of this nearly sacred group. The Protestant theologian Reinhold Niebuhr thought fundamentalists had roots in rural culture and a distrust of reason in favor of emotion.

Back at the gate, my fourteen-year-old self is still trying to decide what to do. The dog is getting increasingly loud. The owner is either not home or dead inside the house, because there is no way not to hear the barking, which has now taken on a shrieking quality. I lift the notebook I carry and pencil in "NOAH" next to the street address. But before I go, I decide to test God.[23] If God wants me to be a saver of souls, God will quiet this dog and let me pass through the gate. I am looking for a miracle, basically, even though I know that's not fair to ask of God—who most likely is pretty busy with other, bigger things.[24] Still, I raise my right hand, as if to part the Red Sea, and the dog stops barking. For a second. And then, as if angered by the brief silence we both enjoy, it starts to throw itself at the fence with renewed fervor. The chain-link bends outward, and the dog nearly collides with me, standing on the other side, in its frenzy to remove me from the premises.

So much for miracles.[25] The dog wins. That day, it—in pro-

23. And I think we all know where testing God usually leads.

24. Here, let us look to the sparrows, and the hairs on my head, all of which God watches over, and knows.

25. As I'd told Pat, the days of miracles were over.

tecting its owner from unwanted guests—serves a higher purpose than mine. And come Judgment Day, when the sinner inside stands before his or her Maker, I will be standing helplessly nearby. I tried to get inside your house, I will say, but your damn dog wouldn't allow it. And God will forgive me that "damn."

Four

A GOOD CHRISTIAN WOMAN

Although we never spoke of it, my family was not always fundamentalist. We started out as members of a Christian church in the dusty little southwest Missouri town of Carterville, where my mother grew up. The pride of the Marrs family reached her majority in the foothills of the Ozarks, met a handsome local man, married him, and bore him three children while trailing him around the world as he doggedly pursued the next rank in his Army career. The military has always been an agreeable option to impoverished young people, and my father was no different. It offered him a way—an understandable, predictable way—of climbing out of the ordinary. I don't think either of my parents understood what climbing that ladder would take. I don't think my mother liked being a sergeant's wife, but I can't fault her for that because I wouldn't have liked it, either.

I am roughly three when news comes that my father is being reassigned overseas. My mother, who gave birth to her two sons in an Army hospital in Munich, loads the three kids into the brown station wagon and drives from Fort Ord, California, back to live with her parents, who do not understand why she is not with her husband and are not shy about voicing their disapproval. To say they are disappointed doesn't begin to address it. My grandparents' worldview was forged in the Depression. You work hard, scrape together some cash, buy a shotgun shack, work some more, and then go home to live with Jesus. You don't trust banks or the government (unless it's FDR[1]). Their code of honor is as solid as the black oaks that dot the hills.

With their marked lack of concern over creature comforts (in the '60s, my mother installed a phone in their house for them, as they saw no need for one), they are like early Christian ascetics. Of all their neighbors, they alone do not push their small town to install a sewer system, and when it comes, they continue to use the two-holer out by the garage, and expect their company to do the same.[2] They eat simply and leave little waste.

Despite this, they don't attend church. When I am old enough to realize that—at age eight or so, when I am already firmly embedded in fundamentalism—I rather admire them for it, even while I fear for their souls' destination.

My mother, who has come to embrace niceties like flush toilets, rather quickly moves from her girlhood home to one of the rather shabby family-owned rental properties. It is a small gray-shingled miner's shack with a porch that lists to the north, a scraggly yard, and the remnants of an outhouse—never used by us. It is the first home I remember. The other homes seem like dreams.

We begin attending the First Christian Church just down the road. The church is similarly named but theologically worlds

---

1. It is only because my grandparents weren't ones to hang photos or pictures (save for the ones that came on the calendar their insurance man sent them every year) that they didn't have on their walls the Holy Trinity of God, Jesus, and FDR. But if they *had* hung pictures? They'd have had those three.

2. But if you think about it, a two-holer is weird. Who wants to sit and chat with someone else during the process of elimination? So even though there were two holes cut in the board, I never once saw two people go in there at the same time. And the one on the right was the one worn smooth by generations of Marrs asses.

away from the denomination in which we eventually land. At First Christian (I don't think there was a Second, but the name was impressive), they have a piano and Christmas pageants. I am a part of one pageant where I must memorize a passage that ends, "Did I say my piece all right?" My mother coaches me to tilt my head to the right at the piece's conclusion and place a finger to my chin—to look coquettish, I suppose. On the afternoon of my performance, she gives me one of those acrid Toni home perms that burns my ears, dresses me in my scratchiest petticoat, and deposits me onstage to do just what she has suggested. I am nervous, and I think my heart is going to stop, but there is a spotlight on me and all else is dark, save for the dim outline of my mother, who is sitting in the front row mouthing my lines with me. I play that last line for all it is worth, and at the end there is a quiet sigh that whooshes through the crowd (that is how I think of them, a crowd, an audience, not members of the elect) and then they clap. This is not a charismatic congregation. No one claps in church, and I am not sure how to react. So I curtsy and get an even bigger hand. The look on my mother's face is well worth the price I will pay later, with my brothers, for being a show-off.

It's a triumph for my mother, pure and simple, and she can use a few victories. She does not want to be in Carterville, doesn't want to be without her husband, isn't patient enough to withstand three boisterous children. She'd imagined a career for herself in advertising, but one semester of Joplin Business College does not a career make. She attached her wagon to my father's star, and when she crashed to earth, I believe she saw her life as all but irredeemable.

Still, I benefit from her dissatisfaction. What she believes she cannot have for herself, she wants for me. When the local school —the school at which she'd garnered so many awards as a student, like cutest of her graduating class—holds a carnival, she enters me into the running as princess, and then she and a couple of her high school friends make and sell mountains of fudge, enough to cover the entire bed of a Ford pickup. The night of the pageant, I wear a cardboard crown studded with glitter. I hardly understand the attention, and I get the sense that the fudge mountain is overkill, but I am glad that my mother is happy.

It must have been frustrating for her, a beautiful, dark-eyed woman with a set of bucktoothed, bow- and hairy-legged children. For my brothers, looks are not so important. It is assumed they will grow into their bodies and faces. But for me, time is of the essence, and an ugly girlhood and adolescence is a deficit from which I can never fully recover. No number of home perms can mask my muscular arms or my flat chest. I know early on that I will always be second-tier pretty when it comes to my mother, and while I reach that realization painfully, I accept it. I do not know how to tell my mother this, so that she can stop being anxious. I know she feels the same disappointment, because when I ask her—as little girls do—if I am pretty, she says, "Pretty is as pretty does." It remains the single most unsatisfying answer of my life.

How trapped she must have felt, the dutiful wife of a soldier with small children. During their separation—and against my father's wishes—she takes a series of factory jobs. And then she sets out to extract herself from her marriage. She writes my father's commanding officer to say that Sergeant Campbell is not sending home money. In fact, he is. She contacts the base chaplain to say her husband is ignoring her. In fact, he isn't, and my father's hard-nosed CO smells trouble. He sends my father home to repair things, but she's met another man at her latest job, a factory where she sews collars onto flannel shirts. He is her supervisor, and the news of his rival hits my father like a fist to the gut. He has never failed before, never done anything but marry the prettiest girl, have three healthy children, and impress his commanding officers.

While he is home on leave, my father fills our kitchen with noise and smells. He makes heaping stacks of corn fritters for his friends—some of whom have visited in his absence and have instructed us to call them "uncle." My father talks loud, dances to the transistor, and livens up the house in a way I couldn't have imagined. I do not know this man, but I love him. I love his bigness. I love his smell. I love that he will burst into song and sing, lustily, "You Are My Sunshine," and expect everyone within the sound of his voice to join in.

And then he leaves, and one day when we are riding to town my mother tries to tell me what divorce means. I scoot forward on the front seat of that bullet-back Ford and press my feet into the floor, seeking an escape. I tell her I wish I'd never been born, and I think I mean it.

I do not like the man she marries when her divorce is final, her boss at the shirt factory. He has been to the house, has taken us to get ice cream, has let me sit in the front seat of his blue Valiant. He tries, but he is not my father, and my brothers and I decide independently to hate him. He is small where my father is huge, dark where my father is light. He is prone to moods. Perhaps my father is, as well. I haven't spent enough time with him to know, but the father I have built up in my mind calls me Daddy's Goil and tells me I'm pretty. The new, reconstituted family moves to Webb City, and we move our church allegiance five miles farther south, to Joplin.

The uncertainty at home sends me swimming fast to the nearest port I can find, the one constant, church, which, things being what they are, now means my stepfather's church. This is not the relatively benign Christian church to which I have become accustomed, but a hard-backed, two-fisted faith that will ask everything of me. There will be no pageants, no opportunities for theatrical stage glory.

And I decide that I love my new church. I love the music and Sunday school and I most especially love Vacation Bible School, where we glue colored beans onto stiff cardboard to form pictures of roosters, and we fashion small churches out of Popsicle sticks and learn songs with hand motions. The failure of my parents' marriage and the onerous presence of my stepfather are pushed aside in those walls, when well-dressed ladies with red lips gather me onto their laps and smiling men in overalls feed me gum, and even though I don't understand what is happening, I feel safe.

I love church, but it doesn't take a biblical scholar to notice that most of the women in the Bible fall into some rather ugly categories. As the youngest in my family and as a girl, I am dedicated to being treated fairly and predisposed to recognize unfairness based on gender, size, or age. With the notable exceptions of women like Sarah, Ruth, Rebekah, and Rachel, I see the Old Testament women as harlots, like Rahab, evil queens, like Jezebel, women who are too beautiful, or women who are ignored and must resort to subterfuge, like Tamar. Bathsheba bathes for King David and look at all the trouble that follows—especially for her poor husband, Uriah, who is sent into battle while the king dallies with his wife.[3]

That women leave such an erratic print across the pages of the Divine Word bothers me, and so when my mother gives me her old Smith-Corona typewriter as a birthday gift, I do at age ten what other, more learned writers are doing elsewhere. I begin to rewrite the books of old, beef up the women's roles, and sell my tales to my doting Grandma Marrs for twenty-five cents a page, which buys me a Butterfinger candy bar as long as my forearm. I am in high cotton, and I and my Grandma Marrs unwittingly join the feminist theological movement, hillbilly branch.

My grandmother pays promptly, but she brags too often, and word gets to my stepfather. He is angry and he tells me to stop. You are not, after all, to change one jot or tittle (the word strikes me as funny) of God's word, and I am changing far more than

---

3. Could there be a bigger soap opera than David and Bathsheba, found in 2 Samuel 11?

that.[4] Thus dries up my first source of income. And again I halt my active search for parity in the Scriptures. I stop, but I am not happy about it.

It is not my stepfather's anger that frightens me so much. I back off of my rewrite for fear of angering God. I like God and I continue to love church. I have no way of believing I'm right when everyone around me tells me I'm wrong. Even my grandmother is chastised when my stepfather confronts us, and my grandmother is rarely chastised.

And there is plenty to distract me. With my youth group, I perform in a gospel puppet team. It isn't easy. Most people instinctively clamp a puppet's mouth shut at each word. You need to open, open, open to let the sound out. My puppet lip-synchs bass.[5] I dip and dive and lower my puppet's head to hit the low notes— all the while feeling the blood drain first from my upraised hand and then from my arm. After a particularly long puppet show, I must slam my hand against the wall in order to get it working again. I like the feeling of numbness and the vague pain of my hand waking up.

We travel to old folks' homes and hide behind a homemade puppet theater and work the mouths of our puppets to recorded hymns. Our arms ache and our timing is off, but most of the members of our audiences are barely awake and tied to their wheelchairs. They are thrilled to hear the old songs—and, to be honest, so am I. The old songs have a majesty to them that newer folksy hymns lack.

When the puppets get too ratty to take out in public, we leave

4. The reference comes from Matthew 5:18. "Jot" in Hebrew is *yodh,* the tenth and smallest letter of the Hebrew alphabet. The tittle is a fancy little fillip at the end of the yodh.

5. I draw my inspiration from my mother's favorite singing group, the Statler Brothers, Johnny Cash's former backup singers. More specifically, I draw on Harold Reid, the bass-singing clown who jokes with the crowd. I and my puppet and our guiding light are all hams.

them behind and sing the songs ourselves: "I'll Fly Away," "Just As I Am" (all three hundred verses), "Old Rugged Cross," and my favorites, "O Thou Fount of Every Blessing" and "A Beautiful Life."

And it is.

But the puppets and the singing and the old people tied to wheelchairs are only a distraction. After being quarantined in the nursery with the babies, I am growing less comfortable with the compromises I've made in my head. I love Jesus, but if all believers are urged to stay on the straight and narrow, there seems to be an especially narrow road built for women.[6] I do not know how to talk about this. I can't ask my mother. I sense she doesn't chafe nearly as much as I do under what are starting to look like very clear restrictions. She has tried to teach me how to get what I want from men—by flattery and subterfuge, mostly—but I haven't the patience for diplomacy and it annoys me that I must go through men to get what I want in the first place. Saying this all out loud will label me in some way I can't yet define. And so I keep quiet.

And then one summer in my teens I vow to read every book in the Webb City Public Library. There I find the story of Elizabeth Cady Stanton.

Stanton grew up the daughter of a wealthy lawyer, under whom she studied and in whose office she learned a powerful lesson. There, Stanton watched desperate women come seeking divorces the law had placed out of their reach. Stanton was a quick study, but that wasn't enough for her father, who once told her that he wished she'd been a boy.[7] Upon that, she applied her-

6. Matthew 7:14.

7. When my brother was brought into the nursery at Fort Campbell, Kentucky, a few days after I was born, he put his little hands up on the window, stood on tiptoes, and said, "Yuck. A girl." A small boy's indiscretion could be excused, but my family loved that story and told it often.

self even more—in school and at Emma Willard's Troy Female Seminary. She grew up, married, and spent her honeymoon at an international abolitionist convention in 1840 in London, where delegates spent less time debating the plight of the slaves and more arguing over whether women should participate in the discussions. The male delegates eventually decided that women could stay—in the balcony, where they were instructed to keep quiet. Stanton moved to her new seat, seething, and there she met Quaker minister and abolitionist Lucretia Mott.

The winds that fanned the flames of the American abolition movement did not stop when the slavery question was decided. Even while slaves were being set free, the next issue facing the country so fractured by the issue of bondage had already seeped into the nation's psyche. Abolitionists—particularly white female ones—noticed that they were battling for their African brothers while some of the same restrictions and bonds laced around their own delicate ankles. The women wanted freedom, too. But some of the very clergy who had fought in the trenches for the rights of African men brought to America by force contended that equal rights for women ran counter to God's will. In 1886, when Stanton tried to directly solicit churches for their support on suffrage, Helen Jackson Gougar, a suffragist and a proponent of temperance from Indiana, argued, saying that such action "has done more to cripple my work [toward obtaining the vote for women]" than any other issue.

When Stanton and her husband, Henry, and their three children moved from busy Boston to the relative middle of nowhere in Seneca Falls, New York, Stanton was beside herself trying to find someone to help her with her growing family. Henry had become a state assemblyman and effectively left her with the kids for months on end. Her marriage may have been a happy one, but the institution as it was interpreted by most people of the day was too small to contain Stanton.

By the time her family had increased to seven children, Stanton told her friend Susan B. Anthony that she had reached her boiling point of domesticity.[8]

Stanton would be a year without paid help in a large home that sat within sight of Seneca Falls' growing industry. On a hot day, the smell of pigs wafted over the river nearby. Seneca Falls was a small burg, By comparison, Boston had theater, ships coming in from faraway lands, and bustle. The only bustle in Seneca Falls rested on the rumps of the women, uncomfortable mesh-wire contraptions that made their hind quarters look extremely extended beneath all those skirts.

Stanton and Mott and others in the burgeoning suffrage movement stayed in touch, and in July 1848 three hundred people—including abolitionist Frederick Douglass—crowded into the Wesleyan Chapel on the outskirts of the village's downtown for a women's rights convention. The ideas put forth at the meeting by Stanton, Mott, Mary Ann M'Clintock, and Jane Hunt were considered extreme and radical. Using the Declaration of Independence as her guide, Stanton wrote—most likely in her upstairs nursery, a back room of her three-wing white clapboard house—the Declaration of Sentiments. Her second paragraph reads: "We hold these truths to be self-evident: that all men and women are created equal; that they are endowed by their Creator with certain inalienable rights; that among these are life, liberty, and the pursuit of happiness." The insertion of "and women" into the Jeffersonian phrase was instructive. It was a match to a tinderbox, and the reaction was swift. To gauge the battle ahead, Stanton began collecting newspaper clippings, the editorial slant of which mostly followed that of the now-defunct *Philadelphia Public Ledger* of September 26, 1848, when it said, "A woman is a nobody. A wife

8. In fact, historians call the period stretching from the 1820s to the 1880s that of the "cult of domesticity," where women's roles were restricted to housekeeping and childrearing. It is also known as the cult of true womanhood, but not in a good way.

is everything." In fact, in the months following the July convention, many of the sixty-two women who signed the Declaration quietly withdrew their names.

But not Stanton. She carried the banner and carried it high. If women were to exist on earth, they would exist as equals to men.

Rather quickly, though, she saw the crux of the matter—which was, in this case, the old rugged cross I'd been singing about. Godly Americans viewed a woman's secondary status as ordained by God, from Eve on. And so, years before liberation theology or feminist theology would do so—and far before Grandma Marrs started paying me for the same work—Stanton sought to reinterpret the Bible. To much controversy, she published *The Woman's Bible*—volume 1 in 1895 and volume 2 in 1898—which looked at verses of the Christian Bible that dealt with women, and sought to reinterpret them. To accomplish this, she had assembled a committee of women interested in suffrage and the Bible; the women were given the task of reading the Scriptures and clipping every verse that pertained to their gender, as well as every verse that noticeably left women out. The verses were then pasted into a blank book and comments were written about each passage.[9] For the 1 Corinthians passage mentioned by my Sunday school teacher, which asked that women keep silent in the assembly, the commentary says: "The church at Corinth was peculiarly given to diversion and to disputation; and women were apt to join in and to ask many troublesome questions; hence, they were advised to consult their husbands at home. The apostle [Paul] took it for granted that all men were wise enough to give to

9. In a foreword to a 1993 edition of *The Woman's Bible,* feminist scholar Maureen Fitzgerald writes: "Stanton often speaks directly to the more conservative suffragists through the pages of *The Woman's Bible,* arguing that their inability to grasp the importance of critiquing traditional religion was either a sign of ignorance or an act of 'cowardice' disguised by talk of political pragmatism and fear of religious opposition."

women the necessary information on all subjects. Others, again, advise wives never to discuss knotty points with their husbands; for if they should chance to differ from each other, that fact might give rise to much domestic infelicity. There is such a wide difference of opinion on this point among wise men, that perhaps it would be safe to leave women to be guided by their own unassisted common sense."

Seeking the vote was one thing. Seeking equal treatment from God was something else again. If public censure was loud against the women who signed the Declaration of Sentiments, it was deafening against *The Woman's Bible*. At the time, suffragists everywhere took a giant step back. Stanton was even censured by her National American Woman Suffrage Association. If suffragists were committed to gaining the vote, they were mostly uncomfortable with taking the idea all the way to the Supreme Being. Gougar said in a suffrage committee meeting in 1886 in Washington, D.C.: "I think it is quite enough to change the National Constitution without undertaking to change the Bible."

Critics decried the work first because of the inherent heresy (so they said) of reinterpreting Christianity's holy text. And then they questioned the work's lack of scholarly review, which bothered Stanton as well. She explained that many scholars were asked for their input but declined for fear of damaging their reputations through association with such an inflammatory work. And, she noted wryly, none of the male scholars she approached had ever once invited a woman's participation in one of their own revising committees, "nor tried to mitigate the sentence pronounced on her by changing one count in the indictment served on her in Paradise."

Stanton and others maintained that their new Bible was meant simply to reexamine Scripture in light of the women who appear in verses that occupy roughly one-tenth of the original book. They wanted to place age-old stories in a modern context in which women played a viable role. Stanton wrote in the introduction, "Come, come, my conservative friend, wipe the dew off your spectacles, and see that the world is moving. Whatever your views may be as to the...proposed work, your political and social degradation are but an outgrowth of your status in the Bible ...How can woman's position be changed from that of a subordinate to an equal, without opposition, without the broadest discussion of all the questions involved in her present degradation? For so far-reaching and momentous a reform as her complete independence, an entire revolution in all existing institutions is inevitable."

Earlier, Stanton had dabbled with revivalism, but after her first exposure to radical politics in 1840s Boston, she never looked back at organized religion. It was, she said, too great a yoke for a woman to bear.

Despite the outcry, much of Stanton's scholarship stands today. There is nothing naive about her work or that of the committee that assisted her, but the thought that God might have intended a more balanced world was too shocking to imagine in the late 1800s and early 1900s. Even Stanton's close friend, Susan B. Anthony, thought her entry into theology ill-advised, although in public she argued eloquently on Stanton's behalf.[10] Still, the National American Woman Suffrage Association distanced itself from the work with a resolution passed in 1896. In part, the resolution said: "This Association is non-sectarian, being composed of persons of all shades of religious opinion, and...it has no official connection with the so-called 'Woman's Bible,' or any theological publication." "So-called" was thought to have been inserted by

---

10. At the 1896 National American Woman Suffrage Association meeting in Washington, Anthony said that for the organization to distance itself from *The Woman's Bible* was to "set back the hands of the dial on reform."

Charlotte Perkins Stetson, also known as Charlotte Perkins Stetson Gilman, a writer of some fame and the grandniece of Harriet Beecher Stowe, author of *Uncle Tom's Cabin*.

Today, you can tour Stanton's simple home—somewhat changed from when she lived there—in Seneca Falls. Closer to the town's center is the National Women's Hall of Fame. When I visit there one summer, long past the days when my own attempt at rewriting the Bible was silenced, the tour guide is new. His ranger cap hasn't come in yet. In thick July heat, he is wearing a shirt of a hot polyester/wool blend and I feel sorry for him. Though small, the museum portrays a world in which women were not considered full citizens. Stanton rightly asserted that much of the discomfort her contemporaries felt about equal rights for women—including the right to vote—stemmed from the fact that the women in the Bible, the country's best-read book, had been markedly ignored, or worse. The indictment women were served in paradise cannot be overlooked, because, let's face it, there's nowhere for a gender to go but up when a culture's creation story involves a woman chatting with a serpent and ushering in work, hunger, shame, mortality, etc.

That's what happens when a woman wants to have it all. All hell breaks loose, and the rest of us pay for it forever. In Sunday school, we were taught to feel for Eve a kind of enmity, but I thought she was only doing what any right-minded woman would do, seeking wisdom. Theologian Anne McGrew Bennett and countless others have returned to the creation story's original Hebrew, which implies that God's actual, untainted idea was for husband and wife to be equal, with no one exercising dominion over the other. As Bennett writes: "It is best not to be too literal in interpreting myths; but it cannot be maintained that woman is inferior even if she was created after man without admitting that man is inferior to the creeping things because he was created after them."

And she returns to the original Septuagint to find that the idea of a man ruling over woman is not God's intention at all.[11] A literal translation reads, according to Bennett: "Unto the woman [God] said, a snare hath increased thy sorrow and thy sighing; Thou art turning away [from God] to thy husband, and he will rule over thee."

"In this translation it is very clear that woman is being warned against depending on her husband rather than on God," writes Bennett. As Bennett reads the verse, God is making an observation, not issuing an indictment. In listening to the serpent, Eve is turning from God, and if she continued on that course, she would end up being not under God's rule but under her husband's. Thus read, the verse suggests that a system favoring men over women is not what God intended, but is punishment indeed.

And still the curse continues. Women who attempt the seemingly impossible feat of possessing a happy and loving partnership; happy children, if they choose to have them; and, these days, employment that feeds their souls risk bringing down the wrath of God. Pity them.

Pity, too, poor Elizabeth. *The Woman's Bible* was moved to the dusty shelves of antiquity. The fierce Stanton died before women gained the vote. Yet despite the problems inherent with a book written by men for men, Stanton—and Susan B. Anthony and others like her—could not break entirely free of the sacred text. Stanton and others who walk the jagged line between faith and reason pay a high price, but people relegated to the balcony and the uncomfortable seats in the back are often those most responsible for moving movements—and religions—forward. We question, therefore we believe. Or maybe it's the other way around.

I get it. I really do. There's comfort to be taken from a hidebound religion. You don't have to ask (or answer) tough questions. God said it (or your pastor told you God did), you believe it,

11. The Septuagint is the original Greek translation of the Jewish Scriptures.

and that settles it. But even from an (unpadded) pew in the back I wouldn't be able to bring myself to frame rigorous examination of the status quo as heresy. I wonder sometimes: if we'd sidestepped our original labeling of Stanton's work as unworthy or worse, if we'd been willing early on to see women as equal partners capable of making decisions for themselves, might we be further along in the discussion?

With this knowledge of women who've come before me—women who squirm in the pews, who ball their hands into fists—I acquire as a teenager the reputation of a smart-ass, though no one calls me that to my face. One Sunday after morning services, I walk past a group of women and overhear one refer to me as a "women's libber." I am pretty sure I know what that means. Those are the women in New York City who burn their bras. I smile inwardly, because I've never even been to New York.

Five

THE THEOLOGY OF SOFTBALL

I grow up playing baseball—not slow-pitch softball, like the other girls, but hardball, like the big leaguers played. In softball, the batter has hours to plan her swing as the pitch arcs (at least six fix in the air) toward her in slow motion. No matter how hard you swing the bat, the sheer weight of the ball retards its passage. There is a ten-run rule. It struck me as a boring game. But baseball—hardball—was lightning fast. We play it first in a lot behind our house, and then, when we move one town over, after my mother marries her second husband, we play at a lot across the street—which is Route 66—from our house. Yes, that Route 66. I am only vaguely aware of the two-lane road's significance, just as I am only vaguely aware that we are hillbillies. The road has a song named after it; an uncle coming to visit from Wichita sings it to us one day. It is not a very good song, but we know enough to cheer when he comes to "Joplin, Me-sou-ree," right between "St. Louie" (we never said it that way, it is St. Lewis to us) and Oklahoma City that supposedly is mighty pretty, but I'd never made it past Tulsa.

Softball is a game I barely pay attention to. It isn't until I am old enough to play organized sports that I learn my official options include and are limited to a large spongy ball around which I can barely fit my fingers.[1]

But that's later. Between the ages of four and eight, I play baseball, where all attention goes to the hard little kernel that stings like hell when it takes an unexpected bounce over your glove and into your lip. And that is where I tend to stop balls when I don't catch them in my first-baseman's mitt—against my lip, which then swells so big I can't breathe through my nose.

So I breathe through my mouth and I keep playing. Something as piddling as a swollen lip doesn't bring me off the field. That would take far more, like the bite of an anaconda—or my Grandma Marrs threatening me from the porch.

Without those distractions, baseball is life and life is baseball. I remember no other activity from my early years before the church of Christ, the church that will come to take up so many hours of the day and night. To both entities, we give our energy and our devotion, and I later discover that swinging a bat is not that different from singing to Jesus. They're both best accomplished if one affects a carefree abandon. If you think too much, you hurt the game.

But our devotion to baseball—my brothers' and mine—differs in one major way from our devotion to Jesus. We freely give our love to baseball, no questions asked. There is no guilt if we don't spend an afternoon playing catch, because we never skip an afternoon playing catch. It does not dawn on us not to play, and

---

1. Honesty forces me to admit that we are a large-handed family. I could palm a basketball when I reached high school, but this was far earlier, when what hangs from the ends of my arms were only moderately freakishly large. And besides, slow-pitch softballs are anywhere from twelve to sixteen inches in circumference. Had I been able to comfortably throw it at age seven, I think I could have bypassed the softball diamond and headed straight to the circus. "See the Ham-Handed Girl!"

when the rains come and the lightning strikes all around, only the angry entreaties of our grandmother can bring us onto the porch to jump from foot to foot until the clouds pass, the sun comes out, and we are free to scream around the bases again. Baseball is the only venue in which we know how to express our rivalries and our love, starting with the ego-crushing choosing up sides for teams. If you are young (like me) and a girl (ditto), you must daily suffer the indignity of waiting until you are chosen for a team, and if you have angered your brothers earlier in the day, you accept that you will be chosen dead last. And if you have particularly angered your brother, the captain, you can be the last one in line and still he will pause before waving you over into his beloved crew, like you are a stray dog that must be fed, even if everyone wishes you would just skulk off into the woods.[2]

The system can work in your favor. If you shine in the eyes of your brother—say, you weather a furtive punch from him and don't tattle—you just might be picked fourth or fifth (but never first). My brothers, though fierce rivals off the field, want most to play on the same team, a begrudging admission of respect for each other. I am the afterthought, but an important afterthought if someone else—someone better on the field than I, which is mostly everyone else in the neighborhood over the age of ten—is being kept indoors for the afternoon. I am nowhere near as good as my brothers, but I can swing a bat and take my place in the lineup. And in the field, I throw myself at the ball with abandon, fat lip and all, with nary any thought given to personal harm.

The injuries we sustain in our hell-bent-for-leather approach to the sport are like small medals we carry: a black eye from running smack into a hedge, a gash on the leg from leaping (but not quite far enough) over a blackberry bush after a fly ball that will not get away. If the price to play is occasionally blood, well, get-

---

2. In the hierarchy of childhood offenses, tattling comes first, followed by wheedling, lying to get out of chores, and hogging the breakfast cereal in the morning.

ting tagged in the mouth hurts enough to serve as a powerful in-
centive not to miss that ball, to stop it where you're supposed to,
in your mitt. It is what I will tell my sons later: You can listen to
me and have it easy, or you can let the world teach you, and the
world is much harsher.

No quarter is asked and no quarter given in the little baseball
field out in back of 217 N. Pine Street, the pre-remarriage residence. My grandparents own the gray-shingled house we live in,
and I don't know the monetary arrangement—if there is one—
between them and my mother.

If things are tense inside that three-bedroom (three bedrooms
more or less, once my grandfather adds my mother's bedroom
onto it) house, life is glorious outside. Out back, blackberry bushes
line the gravel alley, and there is our baseball field, which is just
big enough for an infield. You find your peace where you can. If
as a child you don't know the particulars of a house's unrest, you
are nevertheless attuned to the unease as an amorphous kind of
haunting, a thing in the next room that's waiting to swallow you
up. It serves me to make mine into a definite shape. My bogeyman
lives under the bed in the form of an evil (and silent) witch who is
past her prime. Even at age five, I have been considering the slow-
ing of the human body as it ages. My grandparents are very clear
on this. My grandmother can still crack a single walnut in her bare
hands, but she lets it be known that she is slipping physically.[3] I
only have to hear the story of the house fire once to believe her. My
mother was two, and somehow a fire broke out while my grandfather was off at work, perhaps in the sawmill. My grandmother
was intent on saving her most prized possession, her stove, so she
single-handedly shoved it through the door and out of harm's
way. It was a huge cast-iron model and people were amazed that
one woman could move it so far.

3. Anyone (just about) can crack two walnuts with one hand. Try cracking just
one.

My grandfather walks with a purpose—almost a march in his step even though he's never served in the military. He is in his late fifties and he is ancient. Yet he speaks freely of his more physical days, when he would drive a team of mules between the forest and the sawmill all day, and then come home and plow his family's sorry little garden in Arkansas.[4] Neither grandparent seems particularly upset about their respective imminent demise. It is more like they are just stating fact. In the bloom of youth, you've got it. And then you don't.

Unlike my grandparents, the witch under my bed isn't willing to admit that she is getting slower, and that works in my favor. When I am in bed and I accidentally let an errant hand fall over the side, she sees it, sniffs it, and waits and waits and waits until the last possible moment, when I begin to draw my hand back up onto the bed. Only then does she snatch at it; lucky for me, she is always just a split-second too late.

But I don't trust that witch and I don't trust her arrogance in thinking that she still has it in her to snatch a child's hand at the last possible moment. One day, she will realize that she needs to start grabbing immediately upon seeing my brown little hand hanging over the side, and then I will be sunk, dragged beneath the bed to God-knows-what fate. If God doesn't know, I suspect the devil does.

I must be ever vigilant because the witch haunts my nights and accompanies me during the day. At twilight, I swear I see her huddling in her black dress in the bushes back behind first base. But she never, ever comes onto the field, because if she is anxious to snatch one child (me) under the bed, groups of children—laughing, sweating, happy children—sicken her. If she

---

4. "Sorry little" was how my grandmother described most things she didn't want to brag about. I suspect the garden to which she referred was actually quite lush, as were all her gardens until the year she decided not to plant one. The next year, she decided not to rake leaves. And the year after that, she died.

comes into our midst, she will melt like the meanie in *The Wizard of Oz*. For so many reasons, it behooves us to be happy in the sunlight.

(The one time I try to discuss this with my older brother, he pooh-poohs the idea that it is a witch who haunts us beneath our beds. Instead, he suggests it is turtles that lurk there. I never think to ask my middle brother what is beneath his bed. I am afraid he'll say turtles, too, and I will be outnumbered. That, or he'll say angels, and I will know what I've always suspected: that he is blessed and I am cursed. From then on, I keep the witch to myself.)

Despite her lingering presence, I find my peace out back in the empty lot we christen our baseball field. It is Busch Stadium without the lights, bleachers, concession stand, or outfield. There are no baselines, and bases are more or less dug out of the dirt with the toe of our sneakers. Cass Street is the outfield, as is the alley that separates our lot and that of Otis, the town drunk.[5] That is not an entirely fair description. We are only told Otis is the town drunk. I see no evidence of his drinking, and I suspect he has been turned into the town drunk by my family's gossips who can't think of something nice to say about him. I can. As far as I can tell, Otis is just an old man who lives with his even-older mother, who wears black dresses and old-lady shoes (kind of like witch shoes, but I have no reason to think Otis's mother is a witch, or *the* witch). Otis keeps a vintage hot rod in the red rock garage behind his house. Any ball hit on the garage roof is an out, and Otis is unfailingly cheerful when we ask to scramble up there to retrieve it. I have never seen him drunk, never smelled liquor on his breath, so when my mother starts talking about his inebriation, I keep silent. In our teetotaler house, a beer on the weekend—even a hot,

5. Use of the definite article here may be an affectation on my part. I have no reason to believe that Carterville stopped with just one town drunk, if Otis even was one in the first place. Just sitting thinking off the top of my head, I can name two others, both of whom were in my family.

sweaty Missouri summer weekend after you've mowed your yard —would be considered overdoing it.

The baseball games—which never really end but continue into the next day and the next and the next—are mostly organized by my older brother. This is before his career as an itinerant preacher, back when his devotion and faith belong almost entirely to the St. Louis Cardinals. My brother wants to play for them one day, and no one thinks to tell him that he can't. In the meantime, he fields a team from our ragtag neighborhood (which most days consists of us, Steve Madden, and the dirty Lacey children, whose mother sometimes gets sick in the yard and vomits something white).[6] I am not allowed to play until I prove that I can hold a wooden Louisville Slugger and swing it. I am four when I am finally able to join the roster. It feels like forever.

I don't remember being a particularly good hitter, but I am willing to dive for balls, and scraped knees don't scare me, and so I become something of a fielding phenomenon. No ball gets by me. As fast as my little legs can carry me, I am all over that field. No one has to tell me which one is first base, or where I need to run to next, as I've already stood and watched hours of the game from the backyard, my bleachers.

I love the game, but in truth I am simply trying to blend in, join in, and be a part of my brother's gang. Had he been a trapeze artist, I would have happily climbed a rope to the tallest of swings and launched myself out into the sky. He'd already let it be known that I was not what he'd hoped for when our mother went to the base hospital to deliver yet another baby. It is clear that he wanted another brother to bully, not me. You can bully a little sister but common sense and the threatening presence of parents prevent you from going too far. A little brother has no such protection.

6. In my grandmother's estimation, the Laceys were "filthy as the Mitchells," the Mitchells being a family that once lived in proximity of hers and failed to keep up with her high standards of cleanliness.

But on the baseball field, given the lack of eligible ballplayers, he is able to reach into his heart and find compassion for me, a (yuck) girl. On the baseball field, my gender isn't an issue so long as I can stop a ball and swing a bat.

When my brothers are old enough, they join the local Little League, and for a few years I spend hot summer nights in the bleachers watching them play. I also find fellow travelers at the ball field—other younger siblings who grow up in the dust beneath the bleachers. I cadge money from my mother to go to the concession stand and order a Chick-o-Stick (which, despite the name, contains not one ounce of chicken, but is something like a thick straw of crunchy peanut butter innards surrounded by toasted coconut) and what we call a Suicide—a mixture of all the flavors of soda pop sold at the stand. I love the candy, the pop, and the brightly lit field on which my brothers play. I love the setting sun visible just over the chat piles to the west, and the giant bugs that dive-bomb the lights.

I don't remember being asked, but when I am old enough, I am relegated to the local girls' softball league. It never occurs to me to protest or to try to play with the boys. That will come later. And besides, for the time and place, the local girls' softball league is fairly progressive. We have lights on our field—tall poles that attracted so many bugs that by the end of the evening, they looked like pulsing dandelion puffballs. We have a concession stand. We have people in the stands, fathers and mothers and younger siblings too young to play themselves, ordering their own Chick-o-Sticks and Suicides. At our first practice, I am placed at second base, and almost immediately an aggressive player slides into me, challenging me. I throw down my glove and get into fighting stance. I know how to handle this. You strike back if someone thinks you're weak and then they leave you alone. My quick punch to the stomach has been honed from years in our backyard Busch Stadium. The player who has slid into me is a curly-haired, short, squatty girl who has already lost teeth in a fight; she, too, must have a backyard stadium in her past, because like me she puts up her fists. The horrified coach quickly intervenes and moves me behind the plate, where I will be slid into again and again. He moves me to catcher because I don't cry, but he tells me that I can only stay at the position if I do not strike anyone who slides into me. The best way to fight back, he says, is by playing well.

I know it is wrong to hit, and his rule moves the responsibility for what might be perceived in me as passiveness onto my coach. I could swing a punch, but my coach says no. To be honest, I won't miss making a fist. Besides, I love playing catcher, love that I am a part of every play. I guard home base (and get knocked down). I fire bullets low and outside to second base (where the runner attempting to steal second can be easily tagged). I whip off my mask with great flair to run for foul pop-ups. I even catch a few, and once I lean over a fence to do it. On that play, I rip my jersey and refuse to let my mother patch it because I have earned that flapping sleeve. My teammates applaud me, and a couple rip their own shirts there in the dugout. That my team is rough-and-tumble only adds to the allure. Three of the players are destined for teenage motherhood. One already smokes. But none of that matters once the umpire calls "Batter up!" I no longer have to sit at my brothers' Little League games. I can swing that bat for all I am worth and then run—as Coach says—like my tail is on fire.

I make friends with the curly-haired toothless girl. We are both tomboys, although probably, for the time and place, just about everyone on the team is a tomboy. Today I think we would be known as athletes, not tomboys. My new friend is another girl named Sherri.[7] Like my older brother, she takes great pleasure in removing her partial plate and leaving her fake front teeth where you don't expect them. She is our pitcher, a workhorse who never

---

7. Upon reflection, I had far too many friends named Sherry or Sherri. One, it was a popular name at my school (second only, perhaps, to Debbie). And two, it's like a good haircut. If you find one you like, don't be afraid to repeat it over and over.

whines or misses a game. I know the pitchers on other teams are hotshots. I am grateful for Sherri. She comes away from each game with a uniform only slightly cleaner than mine. And it is a point of honor with me that mine is filthy.

I have my first-ever menstrual period the day of a game, and our uniform includes white shorts. I do not consider missing the game, nor do I worry about bleeding onto my uniform. I have already seen the stupid film at school and my mother has already bought me a big box of sanitary napkins—a name I find funny, because who would buy unsanitary ones? Instead, I sit in the back of our coach's pickup truck with Sherri and tell her my news. She shrugs. She started her period two years ago, she says. It is emphatically not a big deal to her, and so to me it isn't, either. I am relieved that it is not a big deal. I'd been angry that I'd been forced to sit in the gym with other premenstrual girls to watch the stupid film about what it will be like to be a woman—except instead of real people the characters in the film are like cartoons, like Disney characters, blond girls with turned-up noses who brush their long hair in front of a mirror that I expect to contain a witch or something, screeching out at them that it is all a lie, an ugly lie. Womanhood will not be beautiful or my mother would have told me so. As it is, womanhood looks to me like one long bad job capped at the end of the day with children crying out to be fed. And headaches, lots of headaches that force you onto the couch, demanding absolute quiet. There will be no baseball, or even its sorry substitute, softball. There certainly will be no prince. There will be no relief. I sit in the gym and catch only half of what the film is about. Why not tell us what it will really be like?

A few weeks after we sit through the film, and filled with our newfound, half-baked knowledge about menstruation, I am walking to class with a friend when we spy up ahead one of our classmates wearing a yellow dress stained in the back with—horrors!—a touch of blood on the hem. We know where that comes from, and we exchange looks and start to run toward her, but when we catch up neither of us knows what to say. So we say nothing, and hope that someone during the day will have the courage to alert her to the red flag she's waving. If my softball team is nonchalant about menstruation, I am smart enough to know that the rest of the world is far more squeamish. When I am smaller and years from my first period, my own mother refuses to discuss the big square blue box that occasionally takes up room in the grocery cart. Later, when I ask her if I can switch to tampons—so much more suitable for running and jumping—she tells me yes, but that I must learn to insert them myself. This is, after all, "down there," and we don't discuss it. One grandmother calls her private parts her "down yonders," so that when she dies, one cousin jokes that her down yonders were called up yonder, where the roll is called, according to our oft-sung old hymns.

I feel bad that I can't just pretend I'm on the softball field and tell my friend that she's bled onto her dress, but the words are too hard when we're all dressed like girls. Later, I will come to learn the creative euphemisms that describe menstruation, a word we never use. We only say "I am having my period," and then, only if forced and only in whispers. When I stop to think about it—and I do, a lot—"period" is a strange way to describe it. A period ends a sentence. What does the onset of menstruation end? Innocence?

Early on, my relative ease with my body—and the natural maturation process that has taken hold of it, with blood and hair in the strangest places—is in direct correlation to my athleticism. My body has, up to this point, worked precisely as it should to propel me around the bases, to launch me down the basketball court, to lift me up to spike a volleyball over a net. I have learned to trust my body, not to fear it, and certainly not to consider it dirty. I trust that with this new development—bleeding—my body is doing precisely what it is supposed to do. It isn't icky. It isn't gross. It just is. In contrast, my mother tells me of a high school friend of hers who was raised by a maiden aunt who didn't think to warn the girl of the coming flood. The girl discovered her first period in the school bathroom one day, and she gravely announced to her other, more informed girlfriends that she was dying. I'm not sure she ever lived that down. I know she never married, and in my neighborhood that made her an aberration.

My experience is far different. For all of my religion's priggishness about the body and its functions, early on, returning from a game one night in the coach's pickup, someone mentions she is on her period and the conversation goes freely from there to my own comment that I appreciate having a monthly period because it lets me know that things are working. Rather than the eews one might expect from such a statement, I get knowing nods. The body is a temple, yes, but it is also part of the natural world.[8] And so when I start noticing all the advertisements that treat menstruation as a bother and a discomfort, I don't know what to think. Is there something wrong with me that my periods come unbidden and unannounced but right on time? That I don't feel cramps, don't feel moody, don't worry that I've gained ten pounds beforehand? The curse placed on Eve, did it skip me? I am afraid to ask, afraid that it will sound like I am bragging—or being unsympathetic to my stricken sisters who go to bed with heating pads for several days of each month. I worry that I am doing something wrong, but I don't worry much.

Being able to play sports and play them reasonably well puts me in good stead with the boys in my neighborhood, who don't yet want girlfriends, but desperately want someone to play HORSE or bat a tennis ball around with them, or someone who can catch a perfect spiral (or throw one). In my house, being tough and good at sports cuts you some slack. Being feminine gets you nowhere fast, and so I learn to be tough. I sprain every finger and both thumbs multiple times, and I tape them up and keep playing. The important part is finishing the game. Winning is nice too, but if you can't win you at least have to stay on the field, court, or track

8. 1 Corinthians 3:16.

until the sun sets and your grandmother starts calling you through the gloom.

In her 2005 book, *Let Me Play: The Story of Title IX, the Law That Changed the Future of Girls in America,* journalist Karen Blumenthal explores the history of the legislation that opened up athletics to so many of the rest of us, including Donna de Varona, an Olympic swimmer, and profiling Edith Green, the irascible Democrat from Oregon who pushed equality through the halls of Congress.[9] In sports-mad Missouri, we had a decent softball field in a league that stretched back to my grandmother's time, and every school with more than ten students had a girls' track team. A few schools even had girls' basketball—albeit a lame, half-court version of the game. And then came Title IX. The federal government said schools had to offer parity in their educational programs. In school athletics, that meant offering comparable sports for girls that were already offered for boys, but schools like mine initially do little more than give a passing nod to the legislation. My high school doesn't add any girls' sports until three years after the bill's passage. Not until my junior year can we play volleyball and basketball, on two new teams I overhear boys in the lunchroom arguing over. The fear is that the new sports—for girls, no less—will cut into their football or basketball team budgets.

I am a middling basketball player, but I am pretty good at volleyball. I'd never even touched a volleyball until the first practice, but I develop a wicked serve and a lifelong love of the sport. Our coach is our gym teacher, who knows only slightly more than we about the finer points of the game. Nevertheless, we play and learn. We board the bus to go to travel matches. We wear knee pads (if we can afford to buy them ourselves) and our vocal mothers cheer us from the stands. Sometimes they are joined by our

9. Title IX says: "No person in the U.S. shall, on the basis of sex be excluded from participation in, or denied the benefits of, or be subjected to discrimination under any educational program or activity receiving federal aid." Pretty simple, yes?

brothers—only the luckiest of us are cheered on by our fathers, many of whom believe that their daughters' participation in sports is the first step down the road to lesbianism or something worse.

And even if I am not—to my knowledge—considered sexually suspect for being athletic (I suspect that I am, but no one says it out loud), I am advised by one teacher not to throw myself too wholeheartedly into my games as that will render me undatable. A boy wants, she says, a girl he can protect, not a girl who can beat him in basketball. I laugh when she says this, but other than the occasional (platonic) outing with my brother's best friend—a nice young man from church named Forrest—I do not go on a single solitary date until two weeks before my high school graduation. My date is a transplant, a young man who has moved up from Mobile, Alabama, where perhaps they are not as intimidated by athletic women. He is a nice boy, a Southern Baptist, and he asks very little of me. (He didn't need to; I was all over him.)

I suppose the teacher was right. I am undatable.[10]

Still. Playing for my high school's teams is heaven, and because I'm so happy tripping off to practice—regardless of the hour—I don't think about how even though the law is on our side, we're still not given the same opportunities as the boys. I am grateful to be playing at all; I don't want to rock the boat and get into an argument and somehow come off as ungrateful. If we must practice basketball at five-thirty in the morning because that's the only time the gym can be freed up for us, then I will catch a ride in the dark to go play. I will suffer for my sport. Sports is the outlet I understand most, and if we have to do things like wear the

---

10. As I reread what I've written here, this strikes me as such an unscientific conclusion that I am tempted to strike it from the manuscript. Who's to say that it is my athleticism that keeps me from dating? Maybe it's my lousy attitude. Maybe it's the fact that I have two older brothers who've already chased one young man home after school for "bothering" me. That kind of stuff gets around—although I suspect it's my lousy attitude. Or my devotion to Jesus, one.

same uniforms year-round, well, so be it. I am OK with that. I am, at least, when I'm on the field or on the court and I am throwing myself around with the same abandon I once felt on that tiny baseball field out in back of our gray-shingle rental. For me, that year-round uniform is a thick polyester tank top, No. 24, tiny little shorts that would never pass muster at church camp, and my own thick tube socks. It is glorious to suit up.

But I am dimly aware that our high school boys' teams have everything paid for, and the football games they play are heavily attended by fans who, if the game is away, ride on what we call Yellow Hounds, school buses provided by our district. Female athletes are lucky to have a team bus. The boys also have new uniforms for each sport (because, says one coach when I politely mention it, you can't expect a football uniform to double as a basketball uniform, now, can you? But girls can play in the same clothes, be it volleyball, basketball, or track. All you need are shorts and a shirt.)

I find it more curious than wrong, and then one afternoon, Doug, a standout basketball player in my class, steps out of the boys' locker room to show off his new red (school-bought) high-top Converses. I have just been handed my volleyball uniform, which I have dutifully taken home and washed after each match, to wear for our basketball season. Unsuspecting Doug lifts a foot so that we can all admire his new Converses, and I do the only thing I can think to do: I flip him off. I haven't flipped anyone off my entire life except for my brothers, but such a gesture seems entirely appropriate and I don't even mind being sent to the principal's office, where a sad-faced man tells me how very disappointed he is in me that I have set such a bad example. And my being a Christian and all makes it doubly worse, he says. I try to explain, but I get nowhere. I want to tell him that I appreciate the opportunity to play sports, but I don't much like having to arise at 5:00 a.m. in order to have the gymnasium before the boys need it, before the important stuff starts to happen. I try to explain how sick to my stomach I feel getting up that early and then running and pushing myself around the weirdly lit gym. I do my best to explain myself and that flipped bird, but it doesn't matter because he isn't listening anyway. I try once more to explain that it isn't fair that the girls wear the same uniforms all year round, but that falls on deaf ears, too. By year's end, my uniform looks like it has been attacked by cats. I try to steal it when I graduate, but I get caught and have to write an essay, the equivalent of writing "I won't steal school property" three hundred times. Fine. If I am unsuccessful, my best friend Sherry steals the metal baton we pass back and forth in track, so it's all good. When Sherry died of leukemia a few years back, her daughter pulled that baton out of her bag at that Dallas hospital and handed it to me. The baton—beaten and battered—rests on my mantel.

I sit on my couch sometimes and just stare at it. The lessons I learned—particularly in our relays in track—were vital to my growing up. Most of what I am or hope to be, I owe greatly to sports. I am a Title IX baby, and I owe a great deal to the ball, the whistle, and the net. Despite the lack of interest from the decision makers at my school in fully supporting girls' sports, we keep playing. For the inequity that surrounds us, sports is just the thing, and we chant, by our words and actions, "Just give me the ball"—the chance to steal a throw, sink a basket, send a spiked ball to the feet of the opponent, run as hard as we can to break the tape. Just give us the ball, baton, or discus. We'll do the rest. Believe it: there is no stuffing the girl-athlete back into her water bottle. And while I am learning that my body is perfectly fine as it is, that I can do anything I set my mind to, I also learn about unfairness. Watching the inequality in the sports arena makes me more attuned to the inequality elsewhere, particularly at church. The fact that I can't have a new uniform come basketball season is directly tied to my inability to step into my church's pulpit and preach. I just know it.

And then right in the middle of all this musing, my church

hosts an anti–equal rights amendment gathering, and our local state senator—a former speaker of the state house, a man who would hold office in the state senate from 1962 until his death in 1990, who upon his death was described by a colleague as Lincolnesque—shows up to talk about what a shame it would be for our fine womenfolk to have to serve in the foxholes with men during combat. I attend. Of course I attend; if the church doors are unlocked, I am there—and it is my first taste of religion and politics all rolled into one. Never in my memory has my church been so overt in its political involvement. And in that—although we wouldn't have called ourselves such—we are akin to the dispensational premillennialists. The final days are now, and Jesus is coming. If we seek to change the world too much and make it too nice of a place, Jesus won't come again. Better to let things go to hell in a handbasket and hasten his arrival. Getting involved in politics like this—while perfectly acceptable and even admirable on a personal level—just feels wrong as a church community. I am uncomfortable to the extreme, to the point that I realize my hands are balled into fists. The pews are crowded. We opened the doors to like-minded Christians from around the area—not real Christians like ourselves, but certainly ones who saw this legislation as an assault on the American family in general and American womanhood in particular.

If you ever want to make a study of American political debate, the discussion surrounding the equal rights amendment is a good place to start—the polemics, the rebuttals, the fear tactics, and the half-truths. But I am unaware of any of this at the time, and only dimly aware of the ERA—which seems, like so many issues of my day, to be something that affects other people, maybe those hairy-legged, braless women in New York, the ones who insist on marching and making a big deal of stuff I don't understand. Yet if I don't understand all of what is going on, I secretly admire them—while I am still down-home enough to be shocked when a more progressive female classmate wears a T-shirt to school emblazoned with the legend "A woman without a man is like a fish without a bicycle." I appreciate her stance, even while I pity her that now no one will ask her to the prom. If I am undatable, she is untouchable.

All I know at the time is that the blatant blending of religion and politics is shocking and—even worse—I worry that something bad has been done, something irreversible. But no one seems to notice or care. A sin has been committed and no one is doing anything about it. An important line has been crossed, and I am not sure whom to talk to about this. For reasons I can't pinpoint, I do not want an elected official in my sanctuary, and when I think of it that way, that makes no sense, either. Of course politicians should come to church, but this is the first time I have seen one in the pulpit—that most holy place that remains off-limits to me. And this is a topic upon which I have been dwelling most of my conscious life, the idea of fairness. And now here is my church laying it out there, and I come to find out that over all these years the conclusions I've been carefully drawing for myself as a girl are wrong, and I will stand in judgment for them.

I couldn't have been more heartsick if someone announced it from the pulpit: if you take my church's word for it, I, a Christian capable of biblical scholarship far beyond her years, and Bible Bowl champion of Green Valley Bible Camp, am in error.

Six

A WOMAN'S ROLE

At about the time Elizabeth Cady Stanton and friends were beating the drums for votes for women, the social gospel movement was racing through the urban areas of the East, urged on by an outward-facing spirit that had been lacking in earlier church work.

The movement—in which churches concerned themselves with the scourge of matters of the flesh such as prostitution and child labor—sprang from what some historians call the Third Great Awakening in American theology and politics, which began somewhere around 1890 and extended until roughly the start of the Great Depression.

The movement's fervor was palpable. Word spread through a series of come-to-Jesus revivals, starting in rural areas during the rise of evangelicalism in the late 1800s. Like the previous two Awakenings before it, the Third Awakening's revivals were often held out in the open or under large tents with room for thousands of believers, in the most ecumenical fashion imaginable. The normal bustle of villages and byways would slow and even stop while a revival meeting was going on. This might have been due to a general lack of entertainment to otherwise occupy the souls of the towns, but given the crowds, there simply was not enough clergy to attend to the needs of the growing flocks. More involvement from the laity was required, and since women comprised (and comprise) the bulk of church membership, to them fell the duties that a decade earlier would have gone to a man. The acceptance of the induction of women into the clergy—or, at least, into clergy-like duties—came about, then, not because of some seismic shift within the church, but as a simple, pragmatic answer to a growing need for ministers.

With the Third Awakening, revivals had also begun to move into urban areas, where a woman-led zeal for mission work among the poor, the addicted, and the exploited and oppressed was even higher than in rural or small communities. Such situations and concerns existed in rural areas, but the ills of society were thought to be more prevalent in cities, and certainly people were more prevalent there.

By the late 1800s, social reformers had turned their attention most particularly to prostitution, drunkenness, and slavery—all three of which, it could be argued, affected women most directly. Many early suffragists—the forerunners of modern-day feminism—cut their teeth in the abolition movement. And while women were asking for the vote, most of evangelicalism's early adherents would be proponents of the so-called social gospel, part of a movement that would turn Christians into social workers in the truest sense. Evangelicals would work toward prison reform and child-labor reform. They would eliminate prostitution and extend equality to all people.

But for a few minor points of disagreement, feminists and evangelicals seemed made for one another.

Early on, both movements were concerned with individual relationships—evangelicals with the relationship between the person and the Holy, or God; feminists with the relationship between the person and society. In their purest form, both required a marked devotion to a greater idea—feminists to the rights of all;

evangelicals to the sovereignty of God—and, to no less a degree, the inerrancy of the Bible. Early evangelicalism, with its devotion to social justice and reform, pointed to the early church as an example of utopia, or God-on-earth.

Some believers trusted that God was portable and could be brought into the mission fields of the worst slums. Others believed that only by creating separate societies could the culture be salvaged. One of the better-known utopian societies, the Shakers, or United Society of Believers in Christ's Second Coming, developed from the vision of a young married woman, Ann Lee, or Mother Ann, and within the sect, women and men were considered equal. The group emphasized simplicity, but they were perhaps better known for their devotion to celibacy. Members forswore sexual relations and lived in same-sex buildings and practiced chores divided down the gender line. Husbands and wives who joined together would separate at the community gates and treat one another forevermore as brother and sister. At its height in the 1830s and 1840s, Shaker society boasted six thousand members in nineteen communities. Today, only a handful of Shakers survive—though their austerely beautiful buildings can be seen in places like Enfield, Connecticut, near a state prison, and in a more preserved form at Hancock Shaker Village, in Pittsfield, Massachusetts.

But only a few believers saw the necessity of separating completely from the world. Far more evangelicals remained in society to re-create what they thought was an earlier, happier time in an era that was seen as increasingly and perplexingly complex.

Feminists, too, wished to uncomplicate a world of restrictions on women. Feminists, too, spoke of creating a utopia, where men and women of all races were equal.[1]

---

1. Is it not ironic that in the few societies where gender equality was codified—as in the scattered Shaker villages—such equality could be accomplished only by throwing off the ways of the world, including sex? That's another book, entirely.

Before the social gospel revivals swept the country, women had fewer options than men to demonstrate their spiritual autonomy. Their choice of church, spouse, and perhaps family size were the only decisions left to most of them, although the latter wasn't entirely in the woman's control. A male partner could always, by force if necessary, make his wishes known. Evangelical revivals afforded women an opportunity to exercise control in an area that had previously been all but closed to them. Some historians call this the feminization of religion, because women played essential roles as missionaries, seminarians, and ministers. That term, "feminization of religion," resurfaces later as a pejorative, but for a while, at least, for some nineteenth-century women, religion could be used as a tool to chip away at male authority. You can see this in the intensity of both the abolition and the temperance movements.

Certain emerging religions naturally attracted more women than men. Among these were the Quaker sect (where women were admitted as full and participating members of the clergy) and spiritualism. In *Radical Spirits: Spiritualism and Women's Rights in Nineteenth-Century America,* Ann Braude writes that spiritualism —a uniquely American approach to proving the soul's immortality, by carrying on communication with the already dead— demanded an individualistic religious practice rather than one based on position or training. For spiritualists, Braude says, the individual was the "ultimate vehicle of truth," an attitude that opened the doors for less-trained women to assume positions of leadership. This approach to the afterlife was a haven for women who wanted a more liberal approach to theology. While Calvinism, the then-prevalent theology, promoted a marked anxiety about the fate of the soul after death, spiritualism urged the living to link hands with the departed. Spiritualism also held out the radical notion that men and women are equal: perhaps the spiritualists' sense of the permeability between the realms of the dead and living gave them hope that the barriers between the male and female realm were equally porous.

Some historians, however, maintain that a portion of the newfound zeal unleashed in both the abolition and temperance movements can be attributed to the free time newly on the hands of housewives enjoying modern labor-saving devices. The 786-page 1897 Sears, Roebuck & Co. catalog offered countless innovations meant to make a homemaker's life easier (including Dr. Rose's Obesity Powders and a seventy-five-cent reliable cure for the opium and morphine habit). Breakthroughs on the home front included running water, the wringer washtub, stoves, and carpet sweepers. And families were getting smaller. No longer did the average woman have to spend the entire day on the washing. Oh, but that would be too easy and too flip. The women of the late nineteenth and early twentieth century were ripe for a message of equality for all, no matter how their floors were cleaned.

Meanwhile, during its latter-nineteenth-century heyday, evangelicalism was a broad coalition not limited to any one church. Within Protestantism, one could be a Methodist evangelical or an Episcopalian one. By the 1870s, theologians and members of the clergy, like Washington Gladden and Walter Rauschenbusch, were writing the canon for social reform in a social gospel. By the 1890s, while suffragists were pushing for the right to vote, social gospel literature such as the Social Creed of the Churches, and, later, organizations like the Methodist Federation for Social Action, proved that an active approach to God had a hold on the religious world. The social gospel movement—known briefly as Christian socialism—encouraged institutional churches to provide services and recreational facilities for the poor and for new immigrants. According to religion scholar Karen Armstrong, liberal Protestants "tried to baptize socialism." The idea, she writes, was that "Christians should study urban areas and labor problems rather than the minutiae of Bible history, and fight abuses such as child labor."

Evangelical fundamentalism was, in part, a reaction to the social gospel movement. Conservative believers who would later break away to become fundamentalists were first involved in the social gospel movement, although not for the same reasons as their more liberal brothers and sisters. While their concern and passion for fighting against unfair labor practices were just as deep as that of the liberals, the conservatives viewed their efforts as a war against Satan, or, as Armstrong writes, as a "spiritual challenge to the prevailing materialism."

But over time, the differences would slow and stop the glory train. Fundamentalists tended to see the world through dark glasses. Modern-day Puritans, they continually held up society's fabric to spot the inevitable tear. The liberals tended toward believing in solutions. This would figure greatly in later shifts in American theology.

By the time feminism and fundamentalism came to be known as such, the movements were already worlds apart. Despite their early focus on righting social injustice, there wasn't room at the fundamentalists' table for the feminist. Fundamentalists would point to one set of Scriptures to maintain a woman's "traditional" place in society. Feminists such as Stanton would point to others. If there was middle ground, neither camp seemed able to find it.

If fundamentalism and feminism couldn't share a table, most women found the transition from evangelicalism to feminism rather easy. In 1834, for example, the New York Female Moral Reform Society was founded to convert prostitutes to evangelical Protestantism. (The New York chapter would soon be joined by chapters throughout the country.) During the ten years of its publication, the society's journal, *Advocate of Moral Reform,* became the country's most widely read evangelical journal. It was staffed mostly by women, who wrote resolutely, time and again, that contrary to the common wisdom of the time, moral reform was not too shocking to a woman's delicate senses. A July 1, 1838, editorial from the journal adheres to the line of thinking that women and men dwell in separate spheres, yet argues that a woman's sphere is just as important: "If the sphere of woman is distinct from that of man, it is no less important; and in this sphere, her influence is all powerful, either for good or evil. In the contest against licentiousness, our sex must be brought to take common ground against a common foe; their united frown must be brought to bear upon the guilty individual who breaks one of the commands of Jehovah, and tramples under foot the dearest interests of society. Maternal love must be appealed to, maternal vigilance aroused, and maternal influence exerted, to save the rising generation from the pitfalls into which so many who preceded them, have fallen. In this great work, who can act with most propriety and efficiency?"

Well, women, of course. More than a century before mainstream journalism took a cue from them, the staff of the *Advocate* threatened to publish the names of clients of particular prostitutes—a threat that had a noticeable chilling effect on the clients' willingness to patronize those prostitutes.

It was heady work. Women were discovering their public voices and their power. By 1840, 555 similar organizations had formed to combat both prostitution and drunkenness. In that, the women's first taste of victory in the temperance movement gave more than a gentle boost to feminism. For several decades following, the temperance movement was the most important source of feminist thinking in the country. Articles in the organizations' various journals noted the pain caused in families by drunkenness, including the sexual misconduct linked to it. The Woman's Christian Temperance Union could thrive because it allowed women to protest and be activists but also to stay within the confines of home and family. Still, Frances Willard, the second president of the WCTU, was by any measure an outspoken feminist. She advocated separate worlds for women and men, but she also stressed that there should be free movement between those worlds. She pushed for sports for women, and in her 1889 book *Woman in the Pulpit* she argued that the pulpit should be a welcoming place for women. In fact, Willard did much of the work that Stanton would do later. Willard argued against the traditional interpretations of Scriptures that limited women. She affirmed that there were more than thirty passages that urged women to work in public for Jesus, and only two against such work, but those two had no teeth and, if understood in their proper context, really did not restrict women at all. Two years before her death in 1898, Willard said, "I should have loved best of all to be a Gospel Preacher." She would have made a wonderful one.

In addition to Willard, with her book, and Stanton, with hers, a few others within the nascent women's movement turned their eye to the church. Some, like Harriet Livermore, a female minister who called herself the Pilgrim Stranger, preached without stepping outside the boundaries of female subordination. Others —like Willard—were devoted to a more radical egalitariaism. They recognized that the language of Christian servant-hood had been used against them. Those on the underside of history had been socialized into accepting the role of servant to master, thereby serving the politically powerful—in this case, men—and building a system that fed on itself. The result? "We can never draw a clear line between the values 'out there' and the ones we have internalized and embraced as personality-defining," wrote feminist scholar Drucilla Cornell in 1998. "We cannot be the fully original source of our own values, or even know the extent to which we have absorbed conventional morality."

A system that rewards humility and placing others first— with its promise of eternal reward for enduring untenable conditions on earth—invited the oppressed to participate in her own oppression. Add to that the generations of females learning to exhibit qualities that are held up as Christian virtues—such as compassion and empathy—and women are immediately in danger of being taken advantage of. If the literal crux of traditional Christianity holds up as its ideal God the Father's willingness to sacrifice his only Son, how can a woman, already sacrificing her human rights, complain? The traditional notion that suffering is supposed to bring one closer to God predisposed the nineteenth-century woman to participate in her own abuse. Such a notion within legalistic Christianity historically links women to meekness, and yet within the fundamentalist belief system, women also served as the conduit for the original evil in the world, in the Garden of Eden. It was—and is—a losing situation for women. At the same time, as Steve Brouwer, Paul Gifford, and Susan D. Rose write in *Exporting the American Gospel: Global Christian Fundamentalism,* fundamentalist men "seek to control women and the expression of sex, and simultaneously celebrate the status of mother and wife." The power, starting with the segment of population with the least, flows from children to parents, from wife to husband, and from husband to God. So you raise up a few generations of young girls, telling them that they should step to the back of the bus, ingrain that in their psyche, preach it to them from the pulpit, hold up as ideal examples women doing precisely that, and in a few years, you can step back; you need say no more. Your work is done, because you have carefully created a herd of women who know and even begrudgingly accept that their place is secondary, just outside the limelight, clapping for and cheering on the important people who were never taught to put others first.[2]

In my house, the power structure was rarely challenged. My mother was of the generation where you worked (because you had

2. I never understood the role of cheerleaders in my high school. I was friends with them, even belonged to—and led as president—the pep club, but the year I was president, we integrated, opening up membership to the boys. Yeah, it's a small thing, but in sleepy little Webb City, it was a big deal. Why would I board a bus to cheer for boys who wouldn't think of doing the same for me?

to), but not in a career, because a career was something you had planned for and, most importantly, studied for, and few families in my neighborhood had that kind of money. If a family intended to invest in a member's enrollment in college—or trade school —that member would be male. I discovered this when I was graduating from high school and my mother informed me that the family had spent what little money they'd put away for college on my two older brothers.

So you sucked it up and you worked at a job to help put groceries on the table, and then you came home from a long day spent bent (in her case) over an oily sewing machine, with bits of flannel fluff still in your hair, to open up a can of Chef Boyardee and make dinner.[3] And you did so while you slammed pots around, because, frankly, you had three able-bodied children who might have started dinner before you got off your nine-hour shift. But when that is suggested to one of those able-bodied children—the girl-child—she balks. When she is told she will be responsible for preparing one meal a week for the family, she asks which night, and then she asks which nights her brothers will be getting, and when she is told they won't be assigned a night, that they are boys and that they don't need to learn to cook, she erupts.

It is a fine eruption, and one that ends with the handprint of her mother—in red—marked firmly on her left cheek (in the whole family, only her brothers are southpaws, and her mother has a wicked windup). The girl-child runs up the stairs to her bedroom, slams the door, and comes down only for dinner—prepared by her tired and angry mother, who thought to let this one night slide.

It is not unreasonable to ask that growing children—teenagers all—pitch in to help prepare family meals. It is also not outside the realm of possibility that the father figure, the stepfather,

3. There really was a Chef Boyardee, only his name was Hector Boiardi, but that's his real face looking out from the can.

be asked to participate, as well. In fact, knowing that she is pushing it and that the issue of dinner can quickly escalate into hair-pulling fisticuffs, the girl-child suggests that the family divide up the entire week. That is five nights taken care of, and we can all just fend for ourselves on weekends—or go mooch off of friends. It is a fine arrangement, and she has even drawn up a chart to hang on the refrigerator, but when she shows it to her mother, her mother sighs, and says, That is not how this is going to work.

But why? our princess asks. Why don't the boys have to make a meal? They have to eat, don't they? And they will be out on their own one day and they will need to know how to prepare something other than a bowl of Quisp.

Yes, but they will leave home to live with their wives, the mother says, who will prepare their meals for them as I have prepared meals for them up to now. And as you have helped prepare meals alongside me. Our princess continues to argue: That makes no sense. What if no one marries them? What if they must live in an apartment as a bachelor? Will she then be responsible for going to their homes and preparing them meals? What will her own husband say about this?

There is no answer to that, so on her assigned night—was it Monday? Wednesday?—she takes to wandering the neighborhood until it is far past dark and she knows that her mother has tired of waiting for her and is right now slamming pots in the kitchen to prepare something for her hungry menfolk. That is how her mother thinks of the men in the house, as her menfolk, to be spoiled and coddled and spoon-fed like retarded children. There is a payback for this mentality—no one does anything but that they are rewarded for it—but the girl-child can't figure out what that is.

Eventually, of course, our princess disappears for so many nights that she wears her parents down, and she never touches a pot unless she wants to, which she rarely does. (And when she is finally out on her own, she buys five cookbooks and begins to work her way through them, recipe by recipe. Turns out she likes to cook. Turns out, though, she still hates forced labor.) It is a small victory and not one that she relishes, for by avoiding this new chore she is well aware that it falls right back onto the bent shoulders of her mother.

There is no winning here.

Willard wrote: "I believe women should be authorized as ministers in the church of God...man has no greater natural or spiritual rights than a woman to serve at the altars of the church, as minister of the Gospel...If women can organize missionary societies, temperance societies, and every kind of charitable organization...why not permit them to be ordained to preach the Gospel and administer the sacraments of the Church?"

In Illinois, members of the state WCTU presented a petition asking legislators for the right to vote in 1879. The 180,000 signatures were gathered by none other than Willard, then the organization's state president. No less a personage than Susan B. Anthony also began her activist career in the temperance movement. It was one of the first clarion calls for equality in the homes, through a renewed effort to halt alcoholism. Anthony's father, Daniel, a Quaker cotton-mill owner, organized temperance meetings for his workers. Anthony made her first speech at a Daughters of Temperance meeting. She became more interested in feminism when she was turned away as a speaker at a later temperance meeting in Albany. She was told that women were invited to listen and learn, not to speak. Although the WCTU early on embraced the likes of Willard, the more tender members would eventually expel those who tried to overtly push for women's rights.

Such organizations did more than shine a public light on private vices. Historians Geoffrey C. Ward and Kenneth Burns write that the "evangelical zeal of white, middle-class women nullified time-honored distinctions between private activities and public activities normally reserved for men." The suffragette asked for power not based on her family, but on her own ability to effect change. Such a request flew in the face of the doctrine of separate sexual spheres. By 1914, Walter Lippmann would write, in *Drift and Mastery,* that the "awakening of woman is laying the real foundations for the modern world." He continued: "It is no longer possible to hedge the life of women in a set ritual, where their education, their work, their opinion, their love, and their motherhood, are fixed in the structure of custom," adding, "Liberty may be an uncomfortable blessing unless you know what to do with it."

Amen.

The distinction between what was expected of men and of women had existed for centuries, dating back to ancient Palestine, when only a woman of low status left the house to work. So it was a radical change that women of the nineteenth century could as Christian soldiers march off to war against the wages of sin.

But slowly, evangelicalism's emphasis on social reform began to be seen by some of its adherents as its own form of apostasy, or abandonment of the movement's early tenets. The idea that Christians could and should effect social change on a large scale appeared, to some, to smack of theocracy, a blending they could not countenance. The notion of separation began to take hold; fundamentalists within the evangelical movement found themselves focusing more on Jesus's intended return to earth, and they began to view what they saw as society's ills as the scriptural fulfillment of the last days. To try to improve the world was to risk moving into the distance the day of Jesus's triumphant return. Proponents of the social gospel, in the eyes of the fundamentalist, were "making people too much at home in the world," rather than helping sinners be rescued from the world.

About the time the Lyman brothers were publishing their fundamentalist tracts, certain Christians found themselves gradually withdrawing from mainline churches and forming their own groups, but splinters existed even within this newly formed movement. On one side were the more liberal evangelicals, willing to modify somewhat their central doctrines—such as the infallibility of the Bible—in favor of appealing to more potential members.

And then there were the conservatives, those fond of the verse in Matthew: "For many are called, but few are chosen" (Matt. 22:14). That's from a parable about a wedding feast for a king's son that Jesus, near the end of his ministry, was using to teach his disciples. Preferring to see the verse as a statement of fact, these more conservative members of the faith wanted to help things along a little by creating as difficult and restrictive a religion as possible. That was, after all, from the Bible. Gaining heaven shouldn't be easy, and one of the groups most adamant about scriptural rigor was my own church, the church of Christ. By 1906, the census lists the churches of Christ as separate from the Christian Church.

But it wasn't just my church. While some of the faithful were redirecting their energies from the rights of the black man to the rights of woman, a return to what some thought of as the basic tenets of New Testament Christianity was entering into even the most mainstream of Protestant churches. (Roman Catholicism in America was also affected, but given its emphasis on hierarchy, not nearly as much.) Across the board, people wanted what they considered that old-time religion.

The differences between the people who liked their pews padded and those who wanted stiff board might not have been evident to the casual observer. In fact, the transition from Christian Church to church of Christ was fairly smooth in my own family, except that I missed the Christmas pageant. I asked early on why we didn't celebrate Christmas in the style in which I'd become accustomed. After the move to my stepfather's church, my family has a tree, all right, and there are plenty of references to charity and to Santa Claus around the holidays, but it seems odd not to mention Baby Jesus. The Sunday school teacher I ask (the patient one who finally would call my mother to come escort me from the class) explains that we don't celebrate Christmas as a religious holiday because it's never mentioned in the Bible, and we only do things that are mentioned in the Bible. That is the reason, too, I am told, that we don't have organs and pianos, two other elements I miss from my former church services. I remember thanking my Sunday school teacher for clearing the matter up for me.

Again, to the casual observer such a doggedly literal approach to God might seem like so much scriptural hair-splitting, but later, as a young adult, I will teach a Sunday school class, in which I will bring the old stories to life, make them pertinent, give them wings.[4] I will describe characters from the Old Testament as if we'd just sat down and had iced tea together over a long chat. No one knows Ruth or Deborah or David like I do. I am not afraid to talk about the humanity of these people, to make it—this being the '70s and '80s—relevant. And then when those students advance to fifth grade, I will advance with them. It is the bus ministry, only wheel-less. I decorate the walls with flannel renderings of significant Bible characters. I hang balloons. I interrupt my class with shouts of "What are we going to do?" to which my students are taught to respond, "Praise the Lord!" And then the next year, I wait for my assignment to follow these students into sixth grade, and an elder takes me aside to explain to me that I won't be following these students any further, that they have reached the magical moment we know as the age of accountability, at which point they are now responsible for their soul's own destiny. For the girls, I am still a valid resource, but for the boys, well, they need to be taught by a man. Otherwise I run the risk as a woman of usurping authority over a man (1 Tim. 2:11–14), and we can't have that. I ask, voice shaking, if I have nothing of worth to teach a twelve-year-old boy, if he now is in dominion over me. I ask the elder to

4. That sounds like bragging, but it's true. I had a passion for those stories and that was reflected in my retelling of them.

repeat himself—twice—just in case I've heard wrong. I don't re-member the answer. It wouldn't have satisfied me, so I'm sure I didn't listen very closely.

I quickly resign my teaching position. Who needs the head-ache? I remain in the pew, but the shadow grows darker. How can I reconcile my belief in myself as perfectly capable of walking directly to the throne of God with the rules that surround and bind me?

And if I did reconcile all of that, what would God look like?

Seven

A SCARY GOD

As a girl, I laid in bed at night listening to thunderstorms, fearing that the sky would crack open, God would step forth, and I would be found wanting. This wasn't just the musings of a frightened child. I had scriptural reference for it. In Matthew 14, Jesus gets news of the beheading of his cousin, John the Baptizer. It was such a stupid, senseless death, the result of King Herod Antipas promising a young girl—his stepdaughter, Salome, a dancer—anything she wanted. Because John had spoken out against the girl's mother marrying Herod (she'd been the wife of Herod's half brother and there were laws against her marrying a relative of her husband's), the girl had enough family loyalty to ask for John's head on a platter.[1] Herod apparently didn't much want to fulfill his promise, but he'd made it in front of dinner guests, and so John was killed.

(In our fundamentalist upbringing, Salome's back story is lost on us. Instead, we are urged as teenagers to consider what happens when a young woman dances suggestively. Go ahead. Think about it. Need help? When a young woman moves her hips sugges-

---

1. And speaking as a hillbilly? I understand completely the idea of family loyalty.

tively—as she would later in the marital act with her true and betrothed husband—normally right-living men would go off their gourd and do all kinds of stupid things, like order the beheading of a godly man. And so we are not allowed to attend our proms, or dances, or even parties, for fear we will unleash those lethal hips and cause a man to stray.)

(Oh! The power in those hips!)

John's death affected Jesus mightily. After learning of his cousin's murder, Jesus went to a desolate place near the Sea of Galilee, but he couldn't escape the crowds. So he performed a miracle and fed five thousand with five loaves and two fishes, and then he asked his disciples to go ahead out into the sea on a boat while he lingered to pray.

In the wee hours of the morning, a storm arose, and Jesus walked out on the sea to save his friends. The waves were battering the boat, but the pounding water was nowhere near as scary to Jesus's friends as Jesus walking on the water. Peter, who seemed to have been born with something to prove, got out of the boat and headed toward Jesus, but he got scared, started to sink, and cried out for saving. Jesus saved him, of course, even while he chastised Peter for his lack of faith. As soon as the men got into the boat, the wind stopped.[2]

Who could fathom the ways of God or his Son? I thought a lot about those disciples, and how the winds were bad enough, but then up walks Jesus standing on water and the rubber really hits the road. I worried that a similar storm would descend upon southwest Missouri and we would all be battered and beaten, and that on top of all that, Jesus would then step through the tumult and it would all be over but the shouting.[3] I knew enough about

2. Matthew 14:1–33.

3. This is not a particularly southern phrase, despite the Alabama-born writer Rick Bragg's using it as the title for one of his books. It comes from an English tradition, in which a voice vote would be taken (shouted) and then the group would disband.

my own foibles to know that I could hardly expect to be considered worthy of salvation. God would be too exacting—like Santa Claus with a list of who's naughty or nice, but with less bonhomie. I would be found wanting.

The uncertainty of a fundamentalist's place in heaven may be in direct proportion to her uncertainty about earthly matters. We didn't have the confessional and the surety of the Hail Marys like our Catholic friends. Nor did we have the assurance of being saved—a notion enjoyed by our Baptist ones. And so much of what I did, I did out of fear. I knocked doors because I didn't want to go to hell. I gave my old toys to the poor kids because I feared retribution on Judgment Day. I stifled myself when I wanted to gossip because I knew that somewhere, this was all being recorded and that it would surely come back to haunt me.

This is so much about the place where I grew up. Although we felt reasonably comfortable in our Webb City brick rental, with enough food on the table (thanks in no small part to my step-grandparents, farmers who butchered cattle and shared the wealth), we weren't so far removed from the Depression and the grinding poverty that preceded it. Life was tenuous in the Ozarks, and no amount of careful watching of *The Brady Bunch* could reshape the part of our psyches that waited for the tumult. Speaking in the vernacular, we expected to be rode hard and put up wet. Life owed us nothing; our reward would come later (if we proved worthy), in the afterlife, when we would nestle in the arms of sweet Jesus.

If we weren't worried during tornado season about the Big One swooping in from Kansas and casting our meager possessions all the way to Nebraska, we worried about the earth itself. We had earthquakes, and not just small ones. Over on the other side of the state rumbled the New Madrid seismic fault, where a series of the largest recorded quakes ever shifted the course of the Mississippi River in the winter of 1811–12. People up in Quebec felt the tremors.

Imagine living in a world where neither the sky overhead nor the earth below can be trusted to do the right thing. And couple that with the area's history of the most hazardous means of making a living (particularly in terms of the increased risk of lung cancer), iron ore mining.

The iron ore mines had closed two generations earlier, but still we worried about the earth swallowing us up. And besides: if we were no longer threatened with lives spent underground working in the mines, what remained in those caverns and switchbacks still posed a danger. Just across Route 66 was a large abandoned mine that had filled with water. In the summer months, we were warned almost daily not to swim there. Grandma Marrs said the undertow would suck us down and spit us out to California.

Technically, the honeycombs weren't that deep, but we got her drift. Sadly, not every kid had a Grandma Marrs warning them against those dangers, and every spring or so the town would give over a virgin or two, a young man (usually a young man; we young women didn't value having our swimsuits discolored by the deposit-filled water) caught in the undertow while swimming in that unnatural turquoise water.[4] (Water in southwest Missouri is naturally reddish, full of tannin from the falling leaves and various deposits that made some folks rich and others sick.)

And besides, only poor folks swam in the mines. Rich ones went to the creek or the pools. If Grandma Marrs wanted to steer us away from an activity, she would say that it was "plumb tacky," which meant completely tacky. We wanted so badly not to be tacky. At least we, unlike my mother's generation, had television to instruct us in the more couth ways of the world. And here is where shows like *The Brady Bunch* came in handy. I carefully

---

4. The first time I saw Caribbean water, it was precisely the color of southwest Missouri mine water, and I hesitated getting into it.

watched Jan and Marcia to see how they dressed (their skirts were far too short to pass muster at Webb City Junior High, but oh well) and how they interacted with the world. Their passivity was interesting to me—nothing to be emulated, but interesting. Besides, I had my own script.

You can take the hillbilly out of the hills, but the melancholia leaps up and beckons and you must follow, down that dark road beneath the catalpa trees that rain popcorn onto the grass. The religion promises a better home in glory, but says scant little about conditions in the here and now. Alternative-country singer Jim White fought against his own inner hillbilly, but he returned to the Deep South (in his case, the swamps of Louisiana) and gave the uninitiated a short tour in the 2003 documentary *Searching for the Wrong-Eyed Jesus*. Toward the end of his examination of honky-tonks and religion and truck stops and lousy cars, he says, "I was thinking about desperate people here and their . . . hellfire religion . . . Here you feel the presence of the Spirit. You may not like it. It might be wearing a costume of crazy religious people or wild hillbillies or whatever. It's real and it's alive and it's awake. Welcome to Jesus Central." Amen again.

Accordingly, Judgment Day loomed large in my dreams, even if I didn't understand the details of it entirely. Mostly I knew that Jesus would come back and, according to Matthew 25, he would sit on his throne and divide the world into winners (believers) and losers (nonbelievers). The sheep would go on the right, and the goats on the left.[5] I knew sheep and I knew goats and I knew I'd much rather be a sheep.

Of course, by now the term "Judgment Day" has lost its meaning, what with every entity from World Wrestling Entertainment to the governor of California having co-opted it for use in a title, but for a certain breed of fundamentalists, Judgment Day still holds some weight. In addition to Jesus coming back and

5. Matthew 25:33.

the saints being separated from the sinners, as a girl I imagine that we'll all be treated to a short video of our lives, where the high and low points are given equal weight. There will be no context, no "but he pushed me firsts" or anything like that. It will be a movie starring—save for the smallest of supporting roles for our loved ones—us. The horror won't come from the judgment that will follow, but from the knowledge that absolutely everyone who has ever lived will have a chance to view your pathetic, measly little life without the possibility of commentary from you. So you can't explain yourself while the entire world past and present watches you verbally bully someone in an argument. And you can't give the context of why you dropped that dog off in the middle of nowhere, had that abortion, slept with that man (or woman). No, it will be a movie without a soundtrack, without slow mo, without zooming in or point of view save for the All-Seeing Eye, simply your actions up there on the screen. And while you stand quaking and—if you've even a shred of humility—eventually sink to your knees, people can pass their own judgment on you. Maybe we can even add some kind of light board by which viewers can effectively vote you into hell or out of it.

Except that that would rob God of that power, and that power really should belong to God, considering he started it in the first place.

Regardless of who has the final say, the process will be hideous, because even if you give clothes to the poor and tutor immigrants and make a point to drop some money into every cup or bucket extended your way, none of that will balance out the bad stuff. So when the lightning flashes and the thunder rolls, I will curl up in my bed, dreading not my place in eternity but the movie that is my life. In fact, I sometimes wonder if there is a way you can just skip the movie and go straight to hell. On dark and lonely nights, I take comfort that that might be an option.

For all the attention we pay to rules, my particular branch of believers does not hold with the idea of the antichrist, the evil being expected in the last days, who will mislead people mainly because he or she is mesmerizing enough to do so. The antichrist is too amorphous an entity for us, so when our more charismatic brothers and sisters talk about the antichrist, we look at one another and knowingly smile. We muse among ourselves: They obviously are stuck on the jot and tittle of the law, aren't they?[6]

Nor do we buy into premillennialism, dispensationalism, or the religious phenomenon known as the Rapture, a series of understandings for which we must thank John Nelson Darby, an Irish Protestant who as part of the nondenominational Plymouth Brethren is credited with helping create a rather elaborate explanation of the so-called end times—another phrase we don't use regularly—that includes a one-thousand-year reign by Jesus on earth, followed by the judgment and the eventual end of the world.

By comparison, the church of Christ's interpretation of Judgment Day is notable mostly for its lack of details. In Sunday school and in songs that, had we stopped to think about them, would frighten us silly, we are told that Jesus will come unexpectedly, we will all be judged, and then we will be sent to wherever it is thought best we should go. And for most of us, that will be hell.

Read the lyrics:

When the trumpet of the Lord shall sound
And time shall be no more,
And the morning breaks, eternal, bright and fair;
When the saved on earth shall gather over on the other shore
And the roll is called up yonder, I'll be there.[7]

6. And besides, 1 John 2:18 talks about many antichrists coming in the last hour. Things could get confusing.

7. "When the Roll Is Called Up Yonder," written by James M. Black (1856–1938), a prolific songwriter.

Or not.

The hook that sinks into the singer's skin comes from the song's mournful acceptance of a harsh life. It is a dark view of the world, and others notice. We are warned in our songs and in our Scriptures that life will be one long trial, that there will be no letup, and that only through our clinging to the Cross and living as Christly a life as possible do we have a hope of salvation. The best we can expect is to survive this trial with our morals intact, and reach our home in glory to be reunited with our grandparents and parents who've gone before us.

That last notion is for writerly affect. For all the great hillbilly songs about meeting up with Mama once we cross the Great Divide, members of my church know that the circle will emphatically be broken. Many are called, but few will be chosen.[8] We are poor, wayfaring strangers traveling through this world of woe.[9]

Our details of the afterlife involve visions of mansions—a plus for poor folk accustomed to shotgun shacks. We know from Matthew 22:29–30 that Jesus said that after the resurrection there will be no marriage (that's a relief), but that we'd be like angels. On the physical properties of angels, I am mostly unclear, although I am pretty sure they don't have parents. I know angels could wrestle, serve as messengers, and that they fall into categories like cherubim and seraphim. They are smart. They can appear to be like humans. They're not necessarily to be trusted.[10]

And they will be at Judgment Day in droves. So they'll see my movie, too.

To a child weaned on rules and cognizant of just how impor-

8. Matthew 22:14.

9. "I Am a Poor Wayfaring Stranger," a traditional ballad with lyrics of unknown origin.

10. From verses like Matthew 25:41, we know that Satan has angels too.

tant staying in line could be, the church's bare-bones description of our eternities leaves a lot of questions unanswered. Namely:

Would the world both past and present be taken in order of birth? Death? And how long will that take and will there be concessions?

Can we be judged at the same time as our friends and family, so as not to get separated?

Will there be time for a rebuttal?

I yearn so much for something less stark, and the yearning grows with time.

I am a young adult when a woman I will later identify as Julian of Norwich begins to visit my dreams. And yes, I know how that sounds.

In one dream, I am in my front yard gardening, and Dame Julian drives up in a VW Jetta, the make of my favorite car ever. She steps from the driver's side dressed in a flowing blue robe and a white wimple, like Sally Field in *The Flying Nun.* Over her shoulder she has a nice Coach purse. She wears a Mona Lisa smile, and her hands are open and hanging down at her sides. I never see who else is in the car with her, but I think there are others.

Dame Julian comes to me, the skirt of her robe picking up twigs and leaves as she walks. Then, just as she reaches the spot right in front of me, I wake up. I don't know why she is in my yard. (That she arrives in a VW doesn't faze me in the least.) I don't know if I'm supposed to ask her something, wait for her to talk first, or just let things go as they go.

In another dream, my neighbors and I are staging a passion play in the woods across the street from my house.[11] I am perhaps influenced somewhat in this by a trip I once take to Eureka Springs, Arkansas, to view the Christ of the Ozarks, a large white

11. In truth, passion plays don't hold a lot of water with my church.

statue of Our Savior that features a rather sullen line where his mouth should be. It is seven stories high, and—forgive me—it is one of the ugliest things I've ever seen.[12]

But one doesn't just go to the Christ of the Ozarks statue. While there, one must also view the passion play, a two-hour orgy of Christendom that includes hundreds of performers on a tenth-of-a-mile-long stage. It's supposed to be the best-attended outdoor drama in the country. I go with my lone high school boyfriend, the Baptist, and sit spellbound at the spectacle.[13]

I say nothing of this to my neighbors in the dream who are helping me stage the play. Once we have decided who will get to play Jesus—that always goes to a mysteriously handsome visitor of a friend down the street—we start dividing up the other roles. Just as we are in the thick of the argument over who will play the Roman soldiers who cast lots for Jesus's robe, Dame Julian—who has been in the group all along—speaks up. She says, in a voice so deep as to almost be male: "No. That's not how it was at all," and instead of arguing with her—or stoning her, I have those kinds of dreams too—everyone stops to listen.

In the last dream, I am hiking through those same woods and I come upon a Girl Scout troop being led by Dame Julian—again in flowing robes. She is describing for the girls the properties of the plants they are stepping over, and when I fall in to listen from the back, she looks at me and says, in a tone neither accusing nor kind: "What are you doing here?"

This is the closest I will ever get to Dame Julian, a fourteenth-century Christian mystic who reinterpreted God as female back

---

12. But let's not cast stones without knowing our target. The man behind the statue is Gerald L. K. Smith, a closet socialist if ever there was one. Unfortunately, as his life unfolded Smith showed himself to be a racist along the lines of Father Charles Coughlin, one of his colleagues.

13. These days, you can get a premier package for less than twenty-five dollars.

when you could get stoned for harboring such notions. Instead of being stoned, though, she was revered.

At the age of thirty and one-half—Julian is very precise about this—the native of Norwich, England, became gravely ill. During her fevers, her mother came to her side, and a priest administered her the church's last rites. He told her to keep her eyes on a crucifix, and as she reluctantly did (she wanted to keep her eyes heavenward, as that was where she expected to be rather shortly), she had sixteen ecstatic visions of Jesus and Mary. She recovered, and recorded the visions—which she called "showings"—in a short volume and then, after thinking for twenty years, she went back and wrote a longer version of that volume, *Sixteen Revelations of Divine Love*.

An excerpt:

"And thus I saw that God rejoiceth that He is our Father, and God rejoiceth that He is our Mother, and God rejoices that He is our Very Spouse, and that our soul is His loved wife."

She called Jesus "Mother," and equated the pain and anguish of the crucifixion to that of a woman going through hard labor to give birth. For her time, Julian is unique among writers for her interest in discussing the gospel with women in terms they could understand and appreciate.

She became an anchoress, a religious recluse who nevertheless made herself available to give counsel to other Christians —including Margery Kempe, thought to have written the first autobiography written in English.[14] They discussed, according to Kempe, that she was to obey God and listen to her own feelings so long as they didn't corrupt God's word or interrupt her fellow worshippers. (Kempe was known to weep uncontrollably in church, and that must have driven the others crazy.) Julian also

14. Unlike Julian, though, Margery Kempe married and had fourteen children. She spent most of her later life going on pilgrimages, and can you blame her?

said that the Holy Spirit does not condone unkindness, and that the Holy Spirit also moves everyone to chastity. (Against her priest's wishes, Kempe had reverted back to wearing virginal white, despite her numerous offspring.)

Until Julian's death around 1414, she lived in a small cell attended by a handmaiden at the Church of St. Julian in Norwich, opposite a house of Augustinian friars. The cell was destroyed by bombs in World War II, but believers built a replica. Dame Julian took her name from the church, which was named for the patron saint of circus performers and innkeepers.

For anyone who might doubt the legitimacy of her visions, she wrote: "But for I am a woman, should I therefore live that I should not tell you the goodness of God?"

She called herself unlettered and ignorant, although that was probably a literary device more than a statement of fact. Taken as a whole, her *Revelations* have been compared to the work of another great writer, Geoffrey Chaucer. Although she speaks with authority, she was never defiant, for a religious mystic must subjugate herself to her God.

Today, feminist theologians look to Dame Julian's words as touchstones in the movement to reinterpret the Word and world in the way that God most assuredly intended all along. If there are mothers of the movement, Dame Julian is one of them. She let nothing get between her and her God. For years after I leave the church, I wish I could have said the same for myself. I wish I could just believe that God loves women, but the indoctrination I endured at the hands of well-meaning (or so I assume) Christians is difficult to erase. So I must search for believable (and scholarly) counterpoints because I don't quite trust myself. And until I can dissuade myself of the notion that God plays favorites, I cannot honestly sing or pray. Nor can I turn loose of this anger.

Although church bodies—choose a denomination—have traditionally been comprised mostly of women, the hierarchy is populated almost entirely by men. In one study by historian Charles

B. Strozier, among latter-day fundamentalists women accepted "without question" their church's teachings on issues of morality and gender equality (or inequality). Strozier said that the women were quick to identify themselves as scripturally based—and in that sense they differed little from their Puritan mothers, who also showed a deep desire to abide by the law as laid down by the clergy, letter by letter.

I wish Strozier had asked my opinion, but, come to think of it, I doubt I would have said much. I most likely would have re-cited church dogma. There is the story of the frog in boiling wa-ter that one of my sons insists is not true. (I will never know; I haven't the heart to try it.) If you boil a pot of water and put a frog in it, the frog will leap out. If you put a frog into tepid water, turn up the heat, and let the water boil gradually, the frog will stay in the pot until it dies, acclimating to the temperatures until it boils to death. As Grandma Marrs used to say, You can get used to any-thing, including a turd in your hat.

Given a literalist/legalistic interpretation, the writers of the New Testament—at least the New Testament that was popular by the turn of the last century—were capable of astonishing mi-sogyny. We've already looked at the story of the creation of Adam and Eve. In the New Testament, in 2 Timothy 3:6, the phrase "weak women" or "silly women" is used to refer to individuals who are easily misled. The writer is cautioning, addressing the universal "you," against sinning in the last days. There exists be-fore that verse a list of sins to avoid, among them treacherousness, recklessness, and conceit. And then the advice is given to avoid weak or silly women because, in verse 7, these women are "al-ways being instructed and can never arrive at a knowledge of the truth." If this is an admonishment to a particular type of woman, the distinction between them and women in general is not drawn here. And though in its infancy the new Christian movement of-fered an equal hand to women and slaves, the message was lost. According to feminist theologian Mary Daly, Greek satirists of the day often blamed the growth of esoteric cults and superstitions on irresponsible women seeking emancipation. Those weak and silly women are everywhere.

But if the Bible did teach equality of women, wouldn't more churches be ordaining them?

Male disciples of the early church must have felt unsettled about the theological and missionary role of women. Latter-day theologians say that some of the more obviously misogynistic writings of the apostle Paul might have been, in actuality, plants to throw off the ruling powers. Statements that those who knew the Christian faith would see as obvious parody would serve as reassurances to the powers of the day that Christianity was not, in fact, an egalitarian cult and therefore something to fear.

But if such a ruse was in place, no one thought to leave behind some hint for future fundamentalists, who bore into the verses as scriptural and God-sent law to assign women secondary roles in the church and society.

That Paul's work is given such prominence is disturbing. What about John's more egalitarian attitude, which presents New Testament women as viable and active apostles and teachers of the new faith? Surely John was at least as aware as Paul of the tension that women in the leadership aroused in the early church, yet he boldly presented Jesus as approving of women's leadership roles.

The message that Jesus was someone who moved comfortably among women is also lost. Jesus, in his healing of Jairus's daughter in Matthew 9:18–26, showed that he wanted to bring women into the realm of the Holy as well. Healing the young girl, says Lisa Sergio in *Jesus and Woman: An Exciting Discovery of What He Offered Her,* was an example of Jesus's intentionally highlighting the plight of women, but few modern-day writers focus on that. Instead, they use the fallback position of the weak woman in need of rescue—by her Savior, no less. You can't win, can you?

But if the writers who subsequently distributed his words were not willing to risk attention, Jesus's message in regard to women

was downright revolutionary. Jesus simply did not recognize gender in his teachings. Theologian Elisabeth Schüssler Fiorenza calls
Jesus's egalitarian approach to women "inclusive graciousness."

If that message doesn't appear clear in a rereading of the
Scriptures, it is helpful to remind ourselves that the church—and
its writings—did not come into existence until forty years after
Jesus's resurrection. Things got lost. Things got whispered down
the lane. Original meaning could have been abandoned completely in favor of a less egalitarian faith. What else did we lose in
the interim between Jesus and the recordings? And will we ever
get it back?

We want so much to believe in the possibility of purity at
the beginning. What did the authors of our Constitution mean?
What about the authors of our Bible? Is there a Lost Paradise, as
Romanian philosopher Mircea Eliade said, at the pure beginning?
What did we miss by not having someone immediately taking
notes?

But is it only a fundamentalist who worries about the accu-
racy of note taking on the part of Jesus's disciples? Is the detail of
precisely what happened when and who said what really all that
important? If we have the main commandment—to love one another—what more do we need?[15]

Still, the retooling of Jesus's attitude toward women in the
text accurately reflects the times in which the stories were told.
In a world in which an honor-and-shame moral system defined
the culture, the bulk of the shame rested in the feminine world. In
a Mediterranean peasant world, a woman's social position was
equal to that of a child or a slave. Only boys were sent to school, a
situation which only perpetuated a system that limited women. In
Jesus's eyes, people weren't Jew or Greek, slave or free, male or female. They just were, and he loved them.

15. "But now abide faith, hope, love, these three; but the greatest of these is love"
(1 Cor. 13:13).

Admitting that women have a place at the table makes reading the Bible a much more interesting prospect. Mary Magdalene's "demons" might have been anger and resentment that a
society denied her the opportunity to give and to lead, according
to Joyce Hollyday, in *Clothed with the Sun: Biblical Women, Social
Justice, and Us*. Instead, we are told she was a prostitute—a con-
cept found nowhere in the Bible. If we make her sexually suspect,
we know where to put her. In reality, Mary Magdalene, known as
the "sweet friend of God," followed Jesus to the grave, and she appeared to have continued preaching after his death, in what is now
France.

What a lot of time I've spent on this. How much spinning of
wheels, gazing at moonbeams, giving up and walking away for
years on end.

I am reading the writings of Judith Antonelli, whose 1997
Utne Reader article, "The Goddess Myth," sums it up entirely:
"There's a difference between what the Bible actually says and
what men and women say it says. What appears to be sexism in
the Bible is nothing more than a reflection of the sexism that dominated Babylonian, Egyptian, and Canaanite societies..." I am
reading the words of women ministers like Florence Spearing
Randolph, who defied her husband, her family, and her friends
to climb into a pulpit to speak the truth as God told her to. In one
sermon, delivered in the 1930s at her Wallace Chapel AME Zion
Church in Summit, New Jersey, she said, "Fear not, women, because you are about a great work."

I am paying close attention to the writing of Miriam Therese
Winter, a Medical Mission Sister and professor of liturgy, wor-
ship, and spirituality at Hartford Seminary. She wrote *The Gospel
According to Mary: A New Testament for Women,* and *The Chroni-
cles of Noah and Her Sisters: Genesis and Exodus according to
Women*.

I am aching for the message of the Gospel of Mary, a second-
century manuscript that is supposed to reveal a lost tradition of the

leadership of Mary Magdalene, whose opponent was, more times than not, the intractable Peter.

And then I am sitting in a seminary class and I hear Alice Laffey, a biblical scholar and feminist, say, "Many of the texts subvert the hierarchy."

I like that.

Occasionally, I talk about this and many other things with Grandma Marrs, who lets me know by her grunts that this is not a particularly interesting conversation for her. My grandfather converted to Pentecostalism in his seventies. My grandmother, to make him happy, followed his lead. When we talk about God, she speaks in a language I know in my heart. She talks about the Great Mystery, and how things often happen without a reason, and that you usually don't need a reason either. She talks about acceptance. She talks about moving on. It is a little corner of my map home, not "back home," but home. They're right. You can't go back. The grandparents get older and die. Your high school friends join a religious sect that does not allow you access to them. Someone tears down your school, builds a new highway, and replaces the Dairy Creme with a Stop-N-Go, and you're left standing in the housing development that once was your baseball field, trying to remember how everything looked back then. Home isn't there anymore, if it ever really was, and so you'd best be building a new one, one that lasts.

I hold out hope that after all this ruminating, after all these late-night discussions with myself, after all my arm-wrestling with God, I will be allowed to see her face. She will look nothing like me, and when she opens her mouth and speaks in the deepest voice imaginable, she will say: "Darlin'. What took you so long?"[16]

---

16. I don't want to physically resemble her, but I wouldn't mind if her voice sounded like mine.

Eight

THE RELUCTANT FEMALE

It is a goofy picture, and if I'd been thinking clearly I would have thought twice before posing for it. Behind me is the perfectly handsome Rusty, a sandy-haired young athlete who is a year older than I, dressed in his football uniform (sans helmet), smiling broadly, and so far out of my league that to even stand by him on a regular school day, I would need to possess a passport. He inhabits the world of the congenitally popular, whose members seem incredibly at ease in all realms, but most specifically the sexual one.[1] He dates a young woman—also a year older than I— with a flipped-up do and a worldly air. I think she smokes, though I'm not sure of that, and although you don't discuss this in polite company, I'm pretty sure they've Done It. If Rusty were my boyfriend, I would have most assuredly Done It, so I bear neither of them any ill will nor do I mean to judge unduly. Rusty drives a fast car, and from certain angles he looks like a lighter-toned Elvis, before Elvis bloated up like a poisoned puppy.

---

1. While I, on the other hand, worry that my sweaty hands will leave a mark on my skirt. I understood the mechanics of, say, kissing, but had yet to practice on a peer.

I know too much about this couple, from my furtive observations of their entire set, a group that includes Tammy and John and Sherry and Kevin and Rick and Randy. I bear none of them any ill will. Some people are just meant to be popular and cool and it falls to the rest of us to appreciate them.

So why am I here?

Though you can't see it from the camera angle, I am seated in one of those ornamental white metal garden chairs. Resting on my breast is a mum the size of my head.[2] The mum is so heavy and dew-laden that it is pulling my suit coat open in the chill breeze. I am further chilled by the feel of the cold metal on my legs.

My hair is clean and curled and blowing gently. I have loaded it up with what will later be known as "product," but in my time and place was known simply as Dippity-do. So why am I here?

Dangling against my throat is a tiny little silver football on a chain, with the legend SOPH ATT engraved on it, and I figure this is the closest I will ever get to being a Breck Girl. I am the sophomore attendant to the homecoming queen. I have been elected to represent all the girls in the tenth grade in an annual rite I don't understand and only mildly appreciate.

So in the picture, my eyes are crossed.

This is the picture that will be preserved forever, and that is as it should be. As a sophomore in high school I am already enough of a historian to understand that this shot is, after all, an unexpectedly candid portrait of what is supposed to be a serious event. Every season, the boys' sports teams solemnly choose a homecoming queen and her court.[3] The title of queen automatically goes to the senior girl, and the rest of the young women—all in lower

2. I look at my virginity in a time just past the Age of Aquarius with a large dose of ambivalence. Jesus was a virgin, and I love Jesus, but . . .

3. That is, I assume it is a solemn event, but then, I am never in the locker room and for all I know there was no real vote taken. I imagine, looking back, that the girls treated the event with far more seriousness than did the boys.

grades—are considered her attendants. That is what it says on my little football, and on the red ribbon hanging from my over-sized mum: SOPH ATT, sophomore attendant. It is, of course, the gravest of honors to be chosen by an entire sports team to represent them, and to serve as an attendant to the queen. Of course, the title is strictly honorary. We do hardly any attending at all. Nothing much is required of us other than dressing nice, sitting on the back of a convertible without sliding off for a trip around Cardinal Stadium while we wave appropriately (not quite the lightbulb-turning thing a real queen does, but certainly not the floppy wrist action most of us use when we are not hillbilly royalty). And later, after we have been escorted from our cars by hunky football players (mine's Rusty), we will tuck large cro-cheted blankets around our legs (in Cardinal red and royal blue, our school colors) and watch the game from here, a unique advantage over our usual place in the stands.

And after the game, there will be a dance where eight decorated chairs will be set on yet another stage. This is where the queen and her court and their dates will watch over the dance, where—so says my Sunday school teacher—things quickly devolve into an orgy where everyone remains standing and clothed, but writhing all the same.

I can only imagine it, as I have never been to an orgy, nor will I go to the dance. My church doesn't believe in dancing. Or, we believe it exists—only a true fool would deny the existence of dance in the age of disco—but we also believe that the act of dancing bears much of the burden for the breakdown of our society.[4] Young men and women who dance are simply Asking For It, and the It is pretty obvious. Young men and women move quickly from the dance floor to the backseat of a GTO, where the young men seek to deflower the young women. (That there is no de-flowering involved, and that the young women might want to be

4. See "Salome" and "John the Baptizer."

active participants in the sex act, is never, ever discussed. Boys like sex. Girls use sex to get boys, but girls certainly aren't supposed to like it.)

And so my chair will sit empty, as will the chair of my date. I don't have a date, anyway. Why ask a young man to walk me from my convertible to the raised stage on which I'll sit freezing in my short skirt to watch a football game, only to tell him goodnight and go home afterward? I wouldn't burden any boy with that kind of a dud night—not on purpose, anyway.[5] And so I have collared Rusty—or his maybe-a-smoker girlfriend has volunteered him because she knows I need someone to walk me to the stage, and she knows that on that walk—or any walk, no matter how far—I pose absolutely no threat whatsoever. I am the town virgin. Rusty won't be seeking to deflower me. Instead, he will gallantly let me take his arm and he will smile broadly as I teeter on unusually high heels, and then he will gamely go off to play football and never think of me again.

Or maybe he will pity me, once. It hardly matters.

After I am deposited into my metal garden chair, and as I watch the game—the score is lost to the ages—I wonder what my chair at the dance will look like. I wonder if they even bothered to set one up for me and my imaginary date, knowing as they do that the church of Christ has, since forever, taken a strong line against dancing. I wonder, if they did decorate a chair, what it will look like empty up there in the midst of what I imagine is a lot of balloons and streamers and stuff. I don't much miss going to the dance—I don't know how to dance, anyway, and the thought of some boy putting his hands on me fills me with dread. I do not know how those women on television glide so effortlessly in the arms of men, as if they were born there. They don't look nervous

---

5. Although I know one of the boys at church would gladly do the honors, and be completely respectful and wish me well at the end of the night and smile graciously at me at Sunday-morning services. The thought of that sickens me.

or wary at all. They look happy. Do they know that their dancing is leading them straight down the road to the perdition of lasciviousness?

I know that when the time comes, after I am married and in the privacy of our own home, my husband will put his hands on my hips and I will either giggle maniacally (a nervous habit I have) or I will say something bitingly inappropriate and scare the poor bastard off (another nervous habit I have).[6] So if I can put that ugly moment off for another day, I'm comfortable with that. Relieved, in fact. Besides, my parents have arranged to have a bunch of kids from our church youth group come to the house after the game, and then we will all go out for a night of bowling or movies or something equally sexless. It will be my own personal booby prize. I will not be writhing for a man in my new SOPH ATT outfit. I will change into jeans and go be a part of the group, lest my recent success go to my head.[7] You aren't supposed to raise yourself up above the others. I know that. I really do.

Still. Of all the girls—cheerleaders, sluts, and those who walk somewhere in between—the football team has chosen me (me!) to represent the sophomore class as the virgin sacrifice for the big homecoming game. This is a land where high school football constitutes its own religion, where shopkeepers close down for the game, where people whose children have long since graduated and moved away—or people without children at all—load into a fleet of school buses and travel all over the state to cheer for Our

6. Why don't members of the church of Christ have sex standing up? Because they're afraid it might be confused with dancing. Thank you. I'm here all week.

7. More than "I love you," more than "You can do it if you try," my home's credo is, "It sounds better coming from someone else." I can run home and brag about getting straight Es in third grade, and my mother's response will be, "It sounds better coming from someone else." I can hold aloft a trophy I've won in volleyball, and my mother's response will still be, "It sounds better coming from someone else." Later, I will respond, "Yes, but I don't have someone following me home to tell the story of my day, so you'll just have to hear it from me."

Team. This is a big deal. And somewhere in my dark little heart, yeah, the attention is pretty cool.

I also know in my dark little heart that my ascendancy has been aided strictly by the presence of my brother, who is also on the football team. Who is going to vote against me, with my brother—who has his issues, but disloyalty is not one of them—sitting beside them? I am sure he meant well and that when he put my name forward, no one had the nerve to remind him that I am virginal to the extreme and that the attendants and queen in a homecoming court have to be at least a little bit interesting, sexually speaking.

When I ask him—knowing the challenges this honor will present to a God-fearing young woman like myself—why he nominated me, he denies it. He says other boys put my name up and that he remained silent. I think he is lying, but however I got here, I have risen above the other girls, been forced to chat with the rest of the royal court to divine what we will all wear, and suffered my mother, who is on overdrive in her anxious excitement that finally her daughter has arrived at the brink of her own popularity—and that she is a girl, after all. After all those summers spent dusting myself off at the softball field, after the jeans I refuse to abandon and the T-shirts that have become my uniform, I am a SOPH ATT, goddammit. Take *that!* I know my mother has been waiting for this day, and I don't have the heart to tell her that I am not completely comfortable with my amorphous role as whatever-it-is-I-am this chill night. Perhaps because my mother was not raised in the church of Christ, she is still able to see a little gray in the world, but my world is strictly black and white, and placing myself above others as a virginal sacrifice is definitely not a gray area.

But who wouldn't be excited? So I go through the motions. For our outfits, the royal court settles on something practical—skirts and jackets, sort of like office wear, pre-1980s, and I have dutifully gone out and purchased a sedate suit with a flared skirt in a light brown. My mother, I know, had hoped for formals and twenty-button gloves so that I could spend the night feeling like I'm dressed in drag, but the girls—corn fed and practical to a fault—prevail.[8]

For all my discomfort, I actually like the other girls in the court, though I have little in common with them. It is a small school. My class has slightly more than one hundred students. It is hard not to know everyone, but our acquaintance in the homecoming court is the kind where you smile at one another in the hall mainly because you smile at everyone in the hall. It is not a special relationship, nor will it blossom after our shared time in the limelight.[9] I am clear on this and it doesn't make me sad and it doesn't make me yearn to belong to this elite bunch. It is a fact of life. This will be my brief moment in the sun. Of all the members of the court, I expect that I am the lone virgin, and the whole idea of raising the pretty women (of which group I don't necessarily feel a member) above others before a big game, to perch us on the backs of vintage convertibles and drive us around the track so that people can cheer us, feels medieval or worse.[10] I envision a large bonfire (though that's usually not allowed in Cardinal Stadium) on the far end of the field, the visitors' end, into which we, the well-dressed members of the homecoming court, will be

8. "Corn fed" is not considered a slur if it comes from someone who is also corn fed.

9. This is not a cause for regret. I have already been inculcated with the message that a successful person does not stay in the Ozarks. I have further ascertained that the pretty women go west (to star in movies—or, as did a former classmate of my mother's, Jell-O commercials, one) and the smart women go east. I have already determined that whatever looks I have will fade, and so I will rely on my smarts and go east when the time comes.

10. You can go all the way back to Mizpah, the daughter of Jephthah, who promised to God he would sacrifice whatever first greeted him upon his return home from a successful battle. Bad luck for Mizpah, it was she, and she was allowed two months to wander around, and then she was sacrificed, a virgin. Judges 11:29–40.

tossed just prior to the game. This will ensure victory, and the love of football in my hometown is great enough that I believe there are some fans who would actually be OK with this.

Is any other homecoming ATT thinking this? I don't think so. So even on a night when I should be reveling in my woman-liness, I cannot sit comfortably. And I can think of no other protest than to cross my eyes for the all-important picture. (Although I could not have articulated it, I know that by clinging to my vir-ginity—by taking my own, private vow to defend it—I am re-taining a large part of my own power. Although I've never heard it said aloud, I know in my bones that since time immemorial, women who renounce the sins of the flesh are returned, in a sense, to the time before sin when we all were—or so I supposed—equal. As a virgin, I am pre-Eve, pre–fruit of the tree of the knowledge of good and evil. I am sidestepping completely the sweaty back-seats of countless GTOs and Barracudas in favor of my own sex-ual autonomy—or something like that. Anyway, clinging to this makes the nights long but—ultimately—easy.)

I do not subscribe to the notion that a photograph robs you of your soul, but there is something demeaning about being posed for a shot in which you aren't much interested. When I was a little girl, I hated to pose for photographs, of which there were many. Although we were fairly regular churchgoers and the sight of the three of us in little suits (my brothers) and frilly dresses (me) shouldn't have been an occasion to break out the Polaroid, from the pictures in our family album, our Sunday-morning routine went like this: get up, wet hair down to mash down the cowlicks, eat bowl of cereal, brush teeth, change into church clothes, pose in front of house. To protest this, though I would stand perfectly still, I would cock one ankle so that my foot—usually my right one—was not firmly on the ground. I must have known this imperfec-tion would infuriate my mother, but I didn't care. Or rather, I did care, because that is precisely what I wanted to do, infuriate my mother. And so after "change into church clothes, pose in front of house," we could add "infuriate Mom by standing on side of foot." To the untrained eye, such a stance was nothing, but my mother saw, noted the rebellion, and reacted every single time.

So when the picture of the court comes out after homecoming, my mother is angry. How could I spoil such a beautiful moment by crossing my eyes? Is nothing sacred?

I can't tell her that I don't necessarily want to identify as a girl; she will not understand that statement any better than I do. I certainly don't want to be a boy—yes, I love sports, but no, I am not sexually attracted to girls—but I have seen the future as a girl and it looks pretty bleak. Perched there on my cold metal patio chair, the smartest option appears to be to bide my time until the moment feels right to do something, anything, to bring the current situation up short.

A little bit of Mary Wollstonecraft would have come in handy right about now, but it would be years before I read her. In her 1792 *Vindication of the Rights of Woman*, the mother of the author of *Frankenstein* argued that women's plight was the result of their lack of education, and of prejudice. Until women are educated rationally, and are no longer dependent on their husbands, they would be "cunning, mean, and selfish, and the men who can be gratified by the fawning fondness of spaniel-like affection have not much delicacy, for love is not to be bought in any sense of the words," wrote Wollstonecraft.

At the time, it never dawns on me to turn down the SOPH ATT honor, and if I had thought of it, I would not have had the courage to make such a big stink. I don't believe any girl in the history of homecomings in my hometown had ever refused to be seated on the court, and I know it is not just my mother who is enthralled with the custom of showcasing young women before a football game.[11] I know it is citywide, if not worldwide. I had

---

11. I refer here to the Dallas Cowboys Cheerleaders, who had debuted two years before—another reason to hate that team.

forgotten about Laurie Partridge, but she was on television and didn't really count.[12]

So this small act of rebellion, of showing my disdain in a picture, will have to suffice. I know if I play this whole girl-court-worshipping-boy-warriors straight, then I run the risk of next year being named junior attendant, and then senior queen, and I don't want to sit in this metal chair and pose for pictures and wear this ugly-ass mum and act all giddy because you like me, you really like me! ever again.

(That sounds horribly presumptuous, doesn't it? I don't mean that my popularity is a shoe-in. I can fall from grace as quickly as the next person, but in my high school it is pretty much a given that once in the homecoming court, always in the homecoming court. It is strictly a matter of biding one's time and giving at least a nod to staying on the straight and narrow. I would probably have to shoot heroin in the hallway, or show up pregnant, to deflect the crown, and I emphatically don't want to do either of those things, I just don't.)

And so I sit, frustrated beyond belief even while my friends look up at me adoringly. They might as well have been hooting and pointing. It's all the same, as far as I'm concerned. And so I do the only thing I can think of: I spoil the moment with a bit of goofiness that says, This doesn't mean that much to me, without actually saying it. I have remained true to my polite southern roots, and I have not lied to myself either.

Not just my mother is disappointed. It is as if I have stripped down to my panties and paraded myself in front of the entire stu-

---

12. Laurie Partridge, of the '70s TV show *The Partridge Family,* was in one episode named homecoming queen, and used her coronation as a bully pulpit to decry the treatment of a female friend who was denied a spot on the boys' basketball team because of her gender. To her brothers, she said, "All you guys think we're interested in is being cheerleaders or homecoming queens. And then, if we're real lucky, we can all grow up to be Playboy Bunnies."

dent body. My friends don't say much—although I know for a fact that at least two of them are horrified. Instead, I hear from teachers who'd thought, as had my mother, that this would be my coming out, that finally I would abandon my asexual notions and cross on over into Girlville. One teacher tells me she is concerned that I, a good Christian girl, would act in such a manner. That enrages me, but I simply nod. How do you defend yourself when you're not even completely sure why you did something anyway? And what, precisely, does it mean to be a good Christian girl? It is the most damning of phrases, capable of felling the most confident of young women. "Good Christian girl." You either are one or you aren't.

I suffer through a few weeks of ignominy, and gossip dies out as gossip will, and then the next year, the title of JR ATT goes to a different girl, a girl who I think appreciates it, a girl who doesn't squander her place in the lights with a funny face at picture time. Instead, she smiles prettily, her eyes sparkling. And I know she goes to the dance to revel in the attention afforded an ATT.

And good for her. I am never again thrust into the spotlight as a sacrificial virgin, and for that, I am grateful.

Though I manage to elude another stint on the court, the idea of acquiring something more than a pretend date is nudging at me, as a boat will when it's tied to a lake dock. I can hear it knocking, the idea that I should have a boyfriend other than Jesus. Jesus is a spiritually demanding boyfriend, but it appears that most everyone else has a flesh-and-blood one, and I know why. Normal girls have boyfriends. Their boyfriends might not be much to look at and they might not be terribly bright, but they smell like leather and almonds and they wrap their strong arms around you and shepherd you down the hall, a treacherous passage if ever there was one. They open your locker for you and glare at other boys who might come by to taunt or tease you or worse. A girl like me, a girl alone, is vulnerable. Without a big strong (male) arm wrapped around me boys can come up and snap my bra strap (the torture of choice among the less-mature boys in my school). (That isn't really an issue, to be honest. I have already forded that stream. I have simply let it be known that if anyone so much as touches my back—never mind my bra—I will tear their arm off at the root. All one has to do in a small school is let that notion float, tell a few chatty friends, and soon you are left alone. It is a preemptive strike, without the violence.)

Other than for the (platonic) attentions of my brother's best friend, a boy from church, I am a dateless wonder into college. That friend goes away to college and when he is home, he calls me up to go on outings—not dates, really, because while we go to movies and such, we don't kiss. We don't so much as touch. I don't spend a lot of time dwelling on it, unless I am with other girls who dwell on it, and then I happily join in the self-deprecating humor, because that is what is expected. A few of us form what we call the Concave Chest Club, for which we laughingly write bylaws that include a vow to virginity—except, unlike later national efforts like True Love Waits or other abstinence groups, we don't really mean it; we're just seeking to codify our dateless states. Believe me, for some of us, if something even halfway presentable comes along we will take it, and we know it. This is our unspoken vow and it makes far more sense than the virginal one. Let the nuns go without. At some point, I will have me some sex—until, that is, the day I stumble upon stories abut the vestal virgins.

Despite all my reading in my grandmother's attic about Greek and Roman gods and goddesses, the notion that those deities needed something like clergy has escaped me. In the case of Vesta, six women—rare, in ancient Rome, too, that women could be clergy—who led the worship of the goddess of the hearth were chosen when they were between the ages of six and ten. They would then give over the next thirty years of their lives to the worship of their goddess. The women could not come from parents in slavery, and they had to be physically unblemished. (The mind wanders—what might that mean, physically unblemished?) During their tenure, they would tend the sacred fires of Vesta, who was represented by an eternal flame, as opposed to the usual tribute of a statue. They would officiate at ceremonies. A vestal virgin had some influence, though it was considered best kept behind the scenes. No senator would ignore a request from a vestal virgin. They could not marry, but at the end of the three decades, they would be free to reenter the regular world, albeit at an elevated level. They would, for the rest of their lives, be given a place of honor at any public gathering. Upon retirement, they could marry, bear children (if that were possible after the age of thirty-six or so in ancient Rome), and they would be considered a prize catch by any man lucky enough to arrange to marry them. (From all indications, most of the virgins chose not to marry but to remain priestesses.) In short, they would give Vesta their youth and virginity, and she would give them the rest—including freedom from their fathers' rule. Vestal virgins were considered so sacred that if they happened upon a criminal on his way to execution, the criminal would be pardoned automatically.

It strikes me now that had this route been available to me, I would as of this writing be at least eight years into my retirement, getting the best seat in the house and working shockingly little for my own upkeep. Dammit.

I explain to the other members of the CCC the idea of vestal virgins, but no one seems interested. Still, we who are alone nevertheless sit together at games, move as a herd through the hallways, and tentatively create a world where a woman without a man is, well, perfectly able to perambulate on her own.

In her book *Dancing in the Streets: A History of Collective Joy*, Barbara Ehrenreich writes that the Greeks, too, had a special, particularly earthy, sect for women. Although neither Greek nor Roman culture was open to equality between the genders, both offered small loopholes through which women could worship as equals—even as superiors to men. The Romans had their vestal virgins, the Greeks had the god Dionysius, also known as Bacchus.

According to Ehrenreich, women in Greek culture "ordinarily lived in a condition much like purdah," or covered from head to toe and excluded from the power structure. But at the culture's winter dance, the women engaged in what Ehrenreich describes as "a crude pantomime of feminist revolt." They abandoned their cloistered lives, raced to the mountains, donned crude clothing made of animal skins, and danced for all they were worth. Known as maenads, they ran rampant in the woods. They were not drunk, nor were they headed for an orgy—sex being beside the point, as it was, presumably, for their Roman sisters, the vestal virgins.

In all this revelry, they were quite capable of pulling down a deer and eating it raw.

The idea of running through the woods with such wild abandon never occurs to me in high school. Instead, through the lessons we are learning and the societal pressures we are feeling, we come to pay attention to a very different kind of hunt. The world is coupled—heterosexually, of course—and we'd better find a mate but fast. One by one, my girlfriends are finding mates—or suitable representations of same—save for a handful of us who evidently have embraced to our flat chests the bylaws of the CCC. We make fun of our dateless selves before anyone else can, thus deadening the sting. We are the small child laughing hysterically at the run-down carnival, trying to convince herself that this is fun! We're having fun! Our day will come, most assuredly! Our mothers tell us so!

Though what we are to do with that special day is beyond me. A year after I halfheartedly sit as SOPH ATT, a cute young man asks me to the ROTC ball (ROTC being considered far from cool in my school). I have never cared about dancing, but I do care— a little—about this young man, and I actually try to talk my parents into letting me go with him. I have never danced in my life and doubt I would know how and have no reason to believe that

I, like awkward young women in the movies, will step onto the hard floor and magically know the moves to make. No, there will be embarrassment in the offing, but I am willing to risk it because I have been exchanging glances with this nice young man in study hall. We have managed to sit at abutting tables for a month now. He is blond, and his right cheek folds into a beautiful dimple when he smiles. He seems to be a moral young man, and what few words we've exchanged make me think he would be fun to talk to. He is a churchgoer, though not a churchgoer to my church, so his churchgoing doesn't count on any kind of serious level, but at least we know he is open to the idea of God. My brother, who knows him from the football team, vouches for his character. He tells my parents that even in two-a-days, twice-daily practices held in the burning August heat, he has never heard this young man curse.

That would speak volumes in other homes, but my parents say no and they tell me they are disappointed that I have even asked. I should know better than to think I will be allowed to attend a dance. I should especially know what Jesus expects of me. There will be no dances, and no shimmying in a suggestive fashion. I am not to parade my hips for any man save my future husband, and then only on my wedding night.

Their talking like this embarrasses me, and I vow never to ask to do anything fun again. It is just not worth it. Better to shimmy out a window and take matters into my own hands. But I can't very well do that in a ball gown, so I have to tell the cute young man that I can't go, and for the first time in my adolescence, I feel the weight of my restrictions.

I know in my heart that my fundamentalist faith is giving me structure and a purpose. It is the '70s—the Me Decade—and I can look around at the people with whom I have been friends since elementary school and see that they are struggling. They appear to be having a good time, but they are struggling, I know. The tales of their weekend escapades float up and down the hallway every

Monday. During one football game, I am sitting in the pep club section yelling my head off when a friend comes up to inform me that a mutual friend named Terrie is beneath the stands and that she is drinking. I do what any good Christian girl would do. I go find her, pull her by the arm from her group, and ask incredulously what she is doing. To my knowledge, Terrie does not go to church, but she is my friend and I must save her from Satan's pull. She tells me she's only drinking a little bit and that I shouldn't worry about her. She is exceedingly good-natured about this. In my hometown, you grow accustomed to having people question your actions, and you do not take offense—even if the person questioning your actions is a peer. I think I tell her that Jesus loves her, and that I do, too, and that I will worry about her, and worry that my own good example has not been enough. (But on a very real level, I don't necessarily want Terrie to go whole hog, as I have done, because then I will be responsible for her.)

It is a little embarrassing to remember this. It sounds so insufferably self-centered. Do I get extra points for meaning well?

I go back up into the stands but I don't yell so loud because just beneath me is a friend who is going astray. I am thankful that I do not struggle like Terrie. I do not feel a tug to jump into an overloaded car and head over to Galena, Kansas, to drink. Kansas has a drinking age of eighteen and it's far easier as a sixteen-year-old to pass for eighteen in Kansas than it is to pass as a twenty-one-year-old in Missouri. I do not own a fake ID and wouldn't know how to go about getting one. I do not want to see the inside of the famous Green Parrot, the ancient tavern that's preferred by underage drinkers from Missouri. And besides, weird things happen around the Green Parrot that make you wonder. If you're looking for allegories, the land surrounding the Parrot is riddled with abandoned iron ore mines. They snake just beneath the ground's surface, and sometimes the ground just opens up and swallows things whole. Is it strange that a sinkhole recently opened in the back of the building that houses the Parrot and threatened to close the business? In my neck of the woods, that was God trying to re-move a blight from the landscape—until, that is, a structural en-gineer said the addition of pilings in one corner of the building could render it safe. I do not feel like drinking or smoking mari-juana (add that to the list of things that frighten me), and to avoid the issue I simply do not go to the parties that burst like mush-rooms (I do not feel like doing those, either) every Friday. I know that I am called to a higher purpose and I have embraced the boundaries around me for so long that I cannot even imagine step-ping outside of them, except for a little bit.

But when the ROTC lieutenant asks me out, for the first time I want to shake the timbers a little. I am perfectly willing to con-tinue being a good Christian woman, but I can't imagine that I am supposed to dull my senses entirely to do that. Still, I sadly tell him no and he smiles and I look not into his eyes (I think they are blue) but into that beautiful dimple. He says we don't have to go to the dance, that he can just take me on a regular date, no music al-lowed. I almost take him up on this. I really want to spend time with him, but he has achieved a high rank in our ROTC and this dance should be something like his victory lap. So as much as I value the attention and as much as I'd like to get to know him bet-ter, I tell him to ask someone else, and to enjoy his evening, and he does precisely that. We no longer sit next to one another in study hall and we do little more than exchange glances in the hallways between classes. Somewhere I hear a trapdoor slap shut, and the next Sunday I take a look at the young men lined up on the pew up front and I think, "I just can't."

The next time my mother sews a skirt for me, when she pre-pares to hem it I push it low on my hips, like hip-hugging jeans, so that when she pins it, it will be a good two inches shorter than she means it to be. When I am out of eyesight of my house, I will refasten the skirt back around my waist, where it is supposed to ride, and I will, for once, almost look like the other girls who are wearing skirts that barely cover their asses. When my mother questions me on why my skirt is so low, I tell her this is how everyone is wearing their skirts, and she believes me. That, or she knows what I am up to and she decides this is not a battle she wants to fight. Given her history of picking every battle, I suspect this is not the case, and that she is simply too tired or too rushed to understand what I am doing.

My shorter skirts are a small victory, but at least I can show any future young men brave enough to storm the castle that I have legs.

The first time I kiss a boy, I am well past the regular age of experimentation—a high school senior—and he is far beyond me intellectually and sexual-experience-wise. He is a Baptist, a curly-haired boy whom I believe I love. It is a wonderful first kiss and we progress rather quickly to more—stopping just shy of actual intercourse because we both believe we should save ourselves for our respective marriages. I have discovered love, and near-sex, and what no one thought to tell me is that the former is confusing and the latter great fun. That our future marriage probably won't be to one another is something we avoid discussing. Perhaps to hasten the day when we see each other naked, we even get engaged for about an hour.

But at his Sunday school class—attended by many of my friends—a discussion rages as to how far one can go on a date, and my boyfriend says—out loud—that he believes everything up to intercourse is OK. When one of these friends (who, if it can be imagined, is even more sexless than I was before that first kiss) confronts me later, I hardly know what to say. Yes, that is the arrangement I have with my boyfriend, but I hardly thought it would be a topic of public discussion and I am horrified that anyone would think of me in the sex act—or the nearly-sex-act. Jesus did not have sex, did he?

The sins of the flesh are waiting, just around the corner, to ensnare and enslave me. I know that. I have seen it in my own family, perfectly normal-looking people who behind closed doors are carnal to their cores. And I can't be that, I just can't. And so for now it is easier to take a vow that is every bit as binding as that of the Catholic nuns I read about and see on television. (The first time I will actually see a habited nun, I will stop in my tracks and stare, rudely, much the same way I will react the first time I see the Lincoln Memorial in Washington, D.C. For me, the two fell into the same categories—entities that I read about growing up but hardly believed existed until I actually saw them. Years later when I befriend a nun and tell her this, she laughs for a long time. She wheezes that she is not laughing with me, but at me. I don't blame her.)

And so I will step back from the pleasure pit. I will not let him touch my breasts—or my bra. I will not. I just won't. I will not be a tease, either. I overhear my brothers talking about something called "blue balls," and from the best I can understand, the condition occurs when you neck with a boy and don't allow him his release. His balls swell up and turn blue, and eventually the semen backs up into his brain and renders him retarded or worse.

I have always wanted power over someone, but that kind of power scares me. All because of feminine wiles (that is how I have been trained to think of them, as if they are a snake in a basket that you don't want to let out), John the Baptizer got his head chopped off, and scattered around the country are legions of young men rendered retarded because their girlfriends Wouldn't Let Them.

The consequences are huge and the fallout immeasurable. And yet I imagine that sex is fun because everyone is always hinting at it, and the television variety shows that I love so much make it seem so attractive. Even my Grandpa Marrs hints at what attracted him to his first wife, the woman who died of diphtheria, the woman he married before my grandmother. She was pretty, he said, and if this cranky old hillbilly can be drawn to a woman, then sex must be as easy as falling off a log.

My grandmother was one of the church ladies who tried to nurse my grandfather's first wife back to health, but she—Jerusha

—died and left my grandfather and two small children. Jerusha is my shadow grandmother. Tucked into a box of photos is one sepia-colored print of Jerusha, wearing a cloche and standing next to what looks like an old Ford. I don't know if she was tall or short, and the hat casts a shadow over her eyes. In the Bible, Jerusha is only mentioned in relation to her father—Zadok—and her husband—Uzziah, a leper—and her son, Jotham, a popular and godly king of Judah.[13]

So that leaves me—given my limited knowledge of the male psyche—with only one alternative. When my relationship with the nice Baptist dies out, I simply won't date. I will neither encourage nor invite that kind of attention. I will be a sexless wonder, someone who is everyone's friend and no one's lover. I will step away from the trough entirely and eat no more. It isn't as if men have been breaking down the door to get to me, anyway, so it will not be a large loss to the world for me to decline future offers. A few Christian men passing through church might be tempted to ask me out, but I will tell them no. When a young man I meet at church camp comes north ninety miles to my house— uninvited—I am so angry I can barely speak. My mother gamely puts him up on the couch, and when he comes to church with the family, the gossip begins. I am so rude to him that my mother takes me to the side and gives me a stern talking-to. It isn't that the young man is unattractive, but he is screwing up my vows. An uncle who hears of my plight offers to drive to the young man's home to say a few bad words to him, but I decline the offer. Instead, I frost him out.

So save for a few post-high-school young men who don't get the messages I'm sending out, not dating is easy. I know that when I am finally off to a Christian college (most likely Harding College in Searcy, Arkansas), I will meet a fine Christian man and together we will walk one another through the garden. He will call

13. 2 Kings 15:33.

me up and be all nervous and I will be nervous, too, and he will ask me out for a Thursday evening two weeks off, so that I have plenty of time to choose my outfit.[14] The outfit will, of course, be ultrachaste. I want there to be no discussion or confusion as to my purpose. We will go for coffee, perhaps, or bowling. I am a good bowler and I will measure his worth by whether he is miffed that I will most likely beat him. We will do this several times, and finally, maybe on the sixth or seventh date, he will ask if he can hold my hand and I will let him.

We will progress from there to my slipping my arm through his, and maybe we will kiss—lips closed, no tongue—at precisely 10:59 p.m. at the door of my brick dorm. (Having never set foot on the campus of Harding College—now University—I had no way of knowing if it was brick or a pup tent, but that is how I saw it in my head.) We will begin discussions about our future once we decide that we are compatible. I will allow him to touch my breast around this time, and perhaps our kisses will be more fervent.

From there, I'm not really sure what happens. For all the sex that seems to be going on around me, in the movies they mostly just show the man and woman crashing together like two bison, and then the next scene shows one of them waking up with a lazy smile and reaching over to an empty pillow.

Whatever the scenario, we will eventually wake up beside one another in a sheet of crisp, white sheets, but not before there's a minister, two rings, and two crying mothers in the pews.

I almost said "bleachers."

---

14. This is how I envision a date goes, but my ideas have been formed strictly from television and reading *Archie* comic books. Oh, and a Barbie coloring book, where Ken takes Barbie to the Malt Shoppe, spelled just like that.

Nine

STILL, SMALL VOICE

I know from age nine that I will be a journalist, and I choose my career after watching the movie *Teacher's Pet* on television. That film delivered the closest thing to an epiphany I believe I shall ever have. It struck me, as I watched America's virgin Doris Day attract the still-virile Clark Gable, that every female journalist I'd ever seen on television dressed great, talked tough, and didn't take crap off of anybody. This seemed the perfect career for me, and despite the latter-day challenges to America's newspapers—my medium of choice—I haven't looked back.

At my job, I bring to the table a fundamentalist-bred need for clarity, an insatiable desire to pursue the righteous, and yes, the ability to talk tough and not take crap from anybody. Through almost thirty years in the business, and despite the fact that I no longer attend church, I keep rotating back to topics that would concern a religious type. I write about hunger and homelessness, homosexuality and civil rights, the juncture between faith and politics that only rarely is explored in polite conversation. And because I so often write about and around and near religious topics at my newspaper job, I occasionally am asked to speak to civic or faith-based groups. I have three main speeches prepared, canned hams about the portrayal of women in the media (it's not good), the role of a newspaper in a democracy (vital, and I'm not just saying that for job security's sake), and the history of the *Hartford Courant*, where I am a columnist.[1]

These are topics I know to my core, so that I take the written speeches with me when I speak but I rarely have to refer to the text. Especially in regard to the portrayal of women in the media, you'd be surprised how often you can share this message and people still think it's new.

But one day I am asked to give a speech at a local church, a Congregational church, which is like Connecticut's state religion, and I mean that in the best sense. When you see that white spire that anchors one end of a New England town green, it more often than not belongs to a Congregational church. I am not a nervous public speaker. I do not worry about how I look or sound. In fact, I like the attention, but this is a new kind of venue for me, and I try to beg off, plead that my schedule just won't permit it. The man said "speech," but I hear "sermon," and I am not ready.

Throughout my years at Hartford Seminary (and they were several), where I earned a master of arts in religious studies, I assert that I do not feel the call to ministry. I said it, and I mean it. There is no still, small voice that comes to me in the middle of the night. I learned of this voice from a Sunday school story. In the story, the prophet Elijah challenged the prophets of Baal (lord of heaven) and Asherah (queen of heaven)—deities worshiped by Queen Jezebel, the Phoenician queen who helped introduce other gods into the Israelites' world.

Elijah asked the prophets to come to Mount Carmel so that

---

1. First published in October 1764, the *Hartford Courant* is known as the oldest continuously published newspaper in America. Other papers make that claim, but this only makes us more proud. The *Courant* published the Declaration of Independence—on page two. Bad news judgment springs eternal.

their gods could be tested against the Israelites' God. Elijah was alone, surrounded by at least 450 prophets. He set about preparing an ox—as did the other prophets—for a sacrifice. The two groups were to pray to have fire rain down, to light the offering, but despite the efforts of Baal's prophets—praying all day and cutting themselves with ceremonial swords—nothing happened. So Elijah had water poured over his offering three times, soaking the ground beneath it, and then he prayed. A fire fell and consumed everything, including the water.[2]

Elijah ordered the priests to be killed, which angered Queen Jezebel. These were her priests, and Elijah ran into the wilderness surrounding Beersheba, sat down beneath a juniper tree, and asked God to take his life.

Instead, Elijah fell asleep, and an angel awoke him (twice) to prompt him to eat something, and he traveled to a cave where God spoke to him and asked him what he was doing. Elijah, who felt horribly alone, reminded God that he'd done everything asked of him; God sent him to a mountain. There, Elijah watched a great wind that split rocks, and an earthquake that did the same, and a fire, as well.

But God wasn't there. After the fire, though, there was the sound of silence and a still, small voice. That was God.[3]

I love that story, and I know that I have not heard that voice. Still, after all these years, it takes one phone call from a Congregational minister—a man who seems nice enough on the phone—to unhinge me over the prospect of stepping into a pulpit. Certainly, I tell him, a religion as large and diverse as Congregationalism can do better for a Sunday-morning speaker. Surely there is someone better qualified to address the topic of the day, whatever that is. But the minister is gently insistent. He has been reading my stuff for years, he says. He thinks I have something to

2. 1 Kings 18:17–39.
3. 1 Kings 19.

say from the pulpit. I hang up after telling him I will think about it, although I have no intention of doing any such thing.

I go home to talk to my husband about this, but he's no help.[4] He was raised Roman Catholic and, while he would still identify himself as such, he has since found Buddhism. He can't see the big deal of me standing in a pulpit and talking to people. A pulpit is just like a lectern, only bigger. What's the big deal?

And I find I can't explain it to him. There is a vast divide between a lectern and a pulpit. The symbolism of one—authority based on one's own autonomy—in no way compares to the symbolism of the other—authority as granted to the speaker by God.

OK. I know I sound like a nut, trying to explain that because the way was barred for me so long ago, I told myself I didn't want to be in a pulpit anyway. And now an opportunity presents itself for me to climb into the pulpit, and I didn't even work for it, and certainly I didn't ask for it. Like with my earlier vow of virginity, I have, on some level, promised myself that I will never want this (preaching or sex). And, like with my vow of virginity, here is an opportunity to sidestep that promise, made in haste with no real forethought. Here it is.

I am thinking about this far too much, and now what if it turns out that I do want to be in a pulpit? The upheaval in my life will be immeasurable. I will have to quit my job, go back to the seminary—only this time with a real and defined purpose. I will have to become holy. I will have to give up cursing and talking bad about people.

Over the next few days, I find myself picking at a scab I didn't even know I had.

But you've never expressed any interest in being a minister before, my husband reminds me. You went through six years of

4. Surprise! After all the virginal angst, I got married, had a baby, got divorced, floated around a bit, got married again, and acquired a stepson. Yes, I am a mother and a wife. It happens to the least qualified among us.

part-time studies at the seminary and never once heard that still, small voice.

I have a dream that night that lightning splits the roof of that old Congregational church and strikes the good people as I talk. I am hardwired to understand that I don't belong in the pulpit. As big a feminist as I am, I have on some level embraced the limitations set before me. And I fear bucking them. And that makes me both sad and angry.

None of this makes any logical sense, but I know why people who grow up fundamentalist like myself spend the rest of their lives Christ-haunted. Though Roman Catholic, Flannery O'Connor was Christ-haunted. No matter how far she traveled or what she wrote, Christ was floating right by her, about a foot behind, whispering in her ear. One writer says the notion that Christ haunts some of us could be nothing more than our resisting "the stain of modernity." I don't know where I fall on the continuum, but Jesus stands just off to the side. Maybe if we could just maintain a love and a faith in Jesus, all the complexities of the world will disappear and we can return to the garden, the perfect beginning. Things will make sense again. We will know where we stand. It's the uncertainly that is killing us, because we who are haunted are not particularly Christian, yet we can't lose the notion that we should be. He haunts us and at the least provocation—say, an invitation to speak in a church—he rises up in front of us with the most sorrowful look on his face, as if we've been disappointing him all along—which we already knew.

I have never been a fan of people saying "I struggle with that," because it makes daily living sound far too dramatic. But I struggle with this, at my desk at work, at home in my bed, in my car driving back and forth. Can I do this? Should I do this? What's the big deal, anyway?

As far as I'm concerned, I resolve nothing, but the next time the minister e-mails me, I say yes. I don't know why. The answer falls out, unbidden. I think I am tired of being a chicken. I think it is best that I just go ahead and do this and get it out of my system, whatever the outcome, however big the lightning strike and great the number of casualties.

That night, I sit at my computer and compose a sermon, then rip it up, compose a sermon, then rip it up. I all but rest my head on my desk. The words aren't coming—a new phenomenon for me. Trained journalists don't get writer's block. A deadline and a nervous boss and a waiting copy desk and the possibility of a gaping white hole on a newspaper page with one's name emblazoned across it is a powerful motivator to write something, anything. I do not have the luxury in my job of coaxing the right words. I will take any words, provided they come in a timely manner.

And then it hits me. I for whom words—any words—will do just fine am tripping over one particular word, one giant-sized, can't-fit-my-arms-around-it word. I decide to stop calling what I am working on a "sermon." Instead, it will be a lecture, or a speech. That takes the weight off of it; suddenly, I am composing a homey, fireside chat with no import whatsoever. I won't waste my time or the time of the people gathered to hear me speak. We will simply gather to hear me chat, and that alleviates the pressure from this short (fifteen minutes or less) speech/sermon/lecture.[5]

To make sure I don't frighten myself further, I decide not to write out everything I want to say, but to compose notes—talking points, if you will. I will leave myself several roads to go down. I decide to let the Holy Spirit—an entity I don't much believe in anymore and don't much trust—take over.[6] The days fly by.

The morning of my speech dawns sunny and warm. The

5. The funny thing is, I charge myself with keeping it short because I know the membership doesn't like to be held over.

6. As always, I have scriptural reference on this: "But the Helper, the Holy Spirit, whom the Father will send in my name, he will teach you all things and bring to your remembrance all that I said to you" (John 14:26).

church building is about an hour from my house. I leave three hours early, dressed in my version of my Sunday best (pants and a suit jacket and high heels) and before I turn onto the first highway, I have sweated through the jacket. When I arrive with two hours to kill, I drive off into the distance and get out of my car to sit on the grass to pray. Yes, I do. I am not a practitioner of habitual prayer, not like the ones I was taught to pray as a child, addressing the Holy as one would a letter that starts, "Dear God." I am mostly just meditating out loud, asking that I not make a fool of myself, asking that I don't say anything that will harm anyone—but let's be honest, the emphasis is on my pleas not to make a fool of myself. I don't worry much about offending. I have long since learned that my approach to religion will most likely offend someone; I just don't want to hurt anyone. I sit there on the grass (and thereby stain my pants) until fifteen minutes before the bell tolls, and then I drive back to the church.

The ministers—there are two of them, and I get the sense that the one who invited me in the first place has been there the shortest amount of time—are suitably soothing. They tell me I will be fine; they tell me not to worry about the length of my sermon. They do not ask to see what I'm going to say beforehand, which surprises me because if I were a minister and I had me in as a guest speaker, I would certainly want to look over my work. But they don't. We have met beforehand and they trust me more than I trust myself.

I can hear my heart pounding in my head and I honestly think I might faint. I don't have this reaction, as a rule, to public speaking. In general, give me a microphone and I am very happy, but here I am, standing before God and the members of the Congregational church, preparing to fall face-forward onto the nice carpet.

And then I am sitting at the front in one of those chairs that looks like a throne facing the congregation, waiting for my turn to start. By now I've sweated through my pants as well as my jacket. I have written a speech, I remind myself. Or, at least, I have a lot of good leads on one. I sit berating myself that I didn't type out precisely every word I wanted to say, that I honestly thought the Holy Spirit would be interested in the likes of me. Why after all these years would the Holy Spirit make an appearance? I no longer trust myself to wing it but I have left myself no other option. Ha, ha. Silly me. If I had a script—and I desperately want one right about now—I wouldn't trust myself to stay on it. This is going to end badly, I think, and then I run through the scenarios that would be most displeasing, starting with me running off, unable to go on, and progressing to my being overcome with some kind of syndrome that makes me say curse words in public—Tourette's, is it? I wonder what I'll do if someone heckles me. I do not worry about having a comeback. I worry about having a comeback that is clean enough for church people.

The weird thing is, I am never shy and I have never feared hecklers, because they are few and far between, and generally the crowd is on your side, anyway. Only once in my speaking career have I been backed into a corner by hecklers, and that was because there were multitudes of them in a badly behaved crowd that was angry over my newspaper's recent coverage of a local event. There, too, it was a challenge to keep from cursing, but I stayed within the boundaries of good behavior—more so than my audience, anyway.

This is church, I remind myself. Hecklers rarely visit church. The closest thing to a heckler I'll probably see is afterward, when someone will come up to me and quietly berate me. That (again, given my training as a newspaper columnist), I can handle.

The service is going on around me and I need to pay attention—I am trying, I promise—but the voices in my head are getting increasingly loud. This is going to end badly. This is going to end badly—that is quickly replaced by Why did I say yes? Why did I say yes? in a flat-tire rhythm that has to be audible to the faithful watching me from their pews.

And then a quartet quietly stands—all men—and the kind-faced bass singer smiles at me and they sing, for my benefit, "I'll Fly Away." The ministers had asked me earlier if I had a favorite song, and I believe I thought of that one because I like the theme of escape—which I very much want now to do.

The others in the church don't know the words and they're scrambling to find it in their songbooks, but it isn't in there, I bet, because their songbooks look pretty new. What they'll find, instead, are those watered-down peace-mass songs that have absolutely no bite to them, and for the first time I feel a little sorry for them and not just for me. When I visit churches, I make a habit to check the hymnals. If they include "Farther Along," an old hymn if ever there was one, I'm going to enjoy the singing. If they don't, I know that the song service will be something to endure and I will politely hum along to the newer songs that don't seek to twist your heart out of your chest, or scare you to death, or do anything other than give you a chance to practice your harmonizing. A few of the older people are singing along as best as they can on the chorus, but I know every verse, and I am adding my faulty alto to the mix. I am calling up the words of a song I literally have not sung in two decades, and I am remembering every word.

And suddenly, right there in front of the whole church, my heart opens up and I am crying. I am flat-dab crying and I realize with horror that this is something I didn't think to include in my ending-badly list, sobbing in front of the congregation before I even get started. To my credit, I am not sobbing—yet, anyway—but I am crying and I know that the tears are pushing two black mascara tracks down my cheeks. Because my throne is facing the crowd, there is no way to disguise this, and no way to let them know that I will compose myself soon, that they needn't worry that they'll have to sit through fifteen minutes of me blubbering into a microphone. I know I will compose myself, because I've done this before. If I can sit stoically through the most charismatic sermon, the music always does me in. If it is of the old-time hymnals, with a tinge of bluegrass thrown in, I know I am sunk. I will start crying, regardless of where I am or who I'm with. And add to that, after all these years I am here in a church and after all this striving it was just a phone call from a compassionate minister that will put me up there in that dark oak pulpit. And I think how cool it would be if my father—who died more than a decade ago—were here to listen. Even though he was not a churchgoer, I think he of all people would understand what being here means to me. How much would you give to hear your father's voice again?

All that comes crashing down on my sweaty shoulders.

It wasn't an act of God—at least, not like one I'd have expected after all my cogitating. It was just a phone call. So the journey wasn't that difficult, anyway. And what, I think, nearly hiccupping, if this is my still, small voice? I'd been like Elijah, up on the mountaintop looking for God in the wind, the earthquake, the fire. And God just picked up the phone? I fashion a quick prayer: Oh God, let me stop crying and let it be soon. I will be a good person. I will stop gossiping so much (I can't promise to quit entirely, God, sorry). Just let me get a grip here.

I run my suit coat jacket under my eyes and hope that the mascara transfers itself to the dark fabric. I once cried at a son's school concert, in which they sang "Danny Boy," which they also sang at the funeral of my father. I made a vow at the funeral to burst into tears every time I heard the song. Once, it was at First Night in Hartford, and it was played by a quartet of saxophones, if you can imagine that. I was on crutches at the time (ski injury) and I managed to get to my feet and hobble out of there. At my son's concert, I cried and rubbed my face and didn't think anything more of it until I congratulated the choir director, who regarded me with something of a stricken look on his face. I thought I'd interrupted him in the midst of some painful thought.

Later, I went into the restroom and saw that I'd smeared lipstick in two straight red lines up one cheek and down the other. I looked a little like a puppet, with outlines done in red.

So I am aware that I may look like a raccoon, but there's no time to worry about it because the quartet ends, the man singing bass looks at me with another smile, and I take a deep breath and stand up. This is my cue. This is my chance to say all those things that have weighed on me since that long-ago Sunday school class when I asked, in the vernacular, "Why cain't a woman be a preacher?" I have typed my ideas for my speech in fourteen-point font, and double-spaced it. I have not tried to memorize anything, because no one will be impressed by that. These people are used to learned men talking to them. There are no female ministers here—at least, none in the pulpit. And mine is the highest voice they will hear today exhorting them from a position of authority from this pulpit, which is so not a lectern.

I think all of this as I take the three steps toward the pulpit. As with most New England Congregational pulpits, it is somewhat elevated, and I have the sense of looking far down at the congregation, although I think that is a trick my mind is playing on me. I take a deep breath, remind myself to speak slowly, and I begin, with a joke, the one about the guy dying and St. Peter giving him a tour.[7] The punch line—a jab at fun-

---

7. A man dies and goes to heaven and is met at the gates by Saint Peter. They start their tour of heaven, stopping first at a beautiful synagogue with a Star of David on top. "What is that?" asks the recently deceased, and Peter says, "Oh, that's where the Jews go when they die. That's Jewish heaven."

They continue on past a beautiful church with tall spires awash in ornate organ music. "And what is that?" asks the man, and Peter answers, "That's where all good Catholics go when they die."

They keep walking and see places of worship for Muslims, Sikhs, Baptists, and so on, until they run out of pavement and continue down a dirt path through some brush to an open field, where sits a nondescript metal building with no markings whatsoever. "And what is that?" asks the man, and Peter quickly hushes him. "That's the church of Christ," he whispers. "They think they're the only ones here."

damentalists—gets an appropriate laugh, and then I start talking about the crisis in modern Christianity—namely, that we're attached to the rules of the Bible and unhinged and floating free from the spirit of it. It is precisely the kind of sermon that wouldn't fly at the Fourth and Forest church of Christ—at least, not the one I remember. I realize in a panic as I'm continuing to speak that this is not in my notes, per se. In fact, I had wanted to talk about compassion, and here I am going off on a tear about our dogma-encrusted interpretation of Jesus. We all think we know Jesus, but mostly, I say, we use Jésus as a template for our own fears and desires. And in the end, we miss the point entirely.

Where the hell is this coming from? If this is the Holy Spirit, I wish she'd just back away and let me take it from here. I look nervously at my notes, and try to pick up where I meant to be. A few years ago, the Pew Research Center for the People and the Press published a survey that said, in short, that people who tended to vote Republican were more likely to attend religious services regularly than do people who vote Democratic. I mention, then, that I assumed most people in the sanctuary were Republicans, and that I was the last lone pinko left standing. In fact, the Congregational Church is decidedly progressive, in issues of gender politics and in their opposition to the Iraq war. So that gets a laugh, too. I talk about the public face of Christianity, and how it seems to loom largest when confronted with issues that have little to nothing to do with the New Testament's definition of religion (to visit the fatherless and widows in their tribulation, and to keep one's self unspotted from this world).[8] So the historic Jesus probably wouldn't have engaged in discussions about gay marriage or stem-cell research. He simply wouldn't have had the time and he might have considered the conversa-

8. James 1:27.

tions to be a distraction. That's not Christianity. That's just playing with it.

That seems to have become my theme and when I run out of
ways to say that, I thank them for having me, gather up my un-
used notes, and step back from the pulpit. The reaction is polite,
and I don't think I can blame the gathered for that. This is a small
Connecticut church of believers who are trying to be decent people, and I think I have delivered the sermon I most want to give
to my home church. I am far too pedantic, far too willing to throw
down a gauntlet to see if anyone takes it up. They've come looking for the spoken version of their happy hymns, and I've un-
loaded a little fire and brimstone on them—just a taste, I could
have been worse, but still.

But I did it. I stood in a pulpit and I spoke. And not one single matchstick of the roof threatened to fall in.

As for that being a still, small voice, I haven't spoken to a
church since—at least, not during a service. There's a lot of bag-
gage attached to the act, but I believe I have dropped off at least
my carry-on.

For all the thinking I do about church and God and Jesus, I do not
attend church. I am mindful about this; I am purposeful. In other
words, it's a conscious choice not to attend church, even if I don't
feel entirely comfortable with that. Who would, if you grew up
going to church three times a week—more, if the doors were
open? But I would feel less comfortable in a roomful of people
who seem to be missing the point.

Not all Christians, I swear I don't think all Christians are
missing the point, but we have been sidelined and sidetracked for
a couple of decades, if you ask me, from the real point—maybe
longer than a couple of decades, come to think of it.

I am steeped in the culture of Jesus. I watch movies like
Robert Duvall's *The Apostle* and *Tender Mercies* with tears in my

eyes. The idea of redemption is knit into my bones. I believe you can hit the bottom, bounce up, hit it again, and still reach out to hold to God's unchanging hand.[9]

That life doesn't always work out that way renders most of us Christ-haunted folk completely susceptible to nostalgia. We yearn for a faith that isn't, and maybe never was. It leaves us empty, unsatisfied, wanting more. That can turn you mean, but for that, we can hardly blame the rest of the world. Faith isn't delivered like a package, and we who feel nostalgic for something we're missing can't blame anyone else for the lack we feel in ourselves.

I know this in my head. It's my heart that often misses the message.

I am visiting my brother and his family in Missouri. They are hyperinvolved in their church, a Christian church that is similar enough to a church of Christ that I meet them at one of the services thinking I will at least know some of the songs.

After all these years, my brother, the former child star of the pulpit, has ceded the religious upbringing of his children to his wife, a sweet farm girl who is probably a Methodist or a Baptist or something. I honestly don't know. She seems shockingly unconcerned with denominational affiliation and when she says out loud, "Well, it doesn't really matter, does it?" I agree with her with a slight thrill. It doesn't, does it? Their three children go to the church's school, and if they want, my brother tells me quietly, they could be at the church/school every night of the week until quite late, all year long. They have nearly worn a rut in the highway between their farm and the church complex, they are that involved.

And that is the point, I suppose: this church is a family to its families.

For a while, my brother and his wife attended—ran?—

9. From the old hymn: "Time is filled with swift transition. Naught of earth unmoved can stand. Build your hopes on things eternal. Hold to God's unchanging hand..."

a small country church where my brother preached and my sister-in-law played piano. I knew my brother had loosened the reins when he consented to have a piano in a church where he preached, and when he told me about the piano, he kind of shrugged as if to say, What are you going to do? or, It doesn't really matter, does it? That particular visit was too short for me to explain that I had stopped caring about what accompanies church hymns a long time ago, that I had stopped attending church altogether. So I just agreed.

Their church complex is set on a hill near a local college, and for all his boyhood zeal, now my brother seems content to take his family to its various activities, and sit up high in the bleachers when he is supposed to sit, and stand when he is supposed to stand to wanly sing along with the hymns whose lyrics are broadcast on a big screen overhead of the pulpit. He is not a deacon, or an elder, or any other kind of official in this smallish megachurch, as far as I can see.

At the service, the song leader cues the small band—a keyboardist, a drummer, and two guitarists—and my brother bends to warn me: "This is Religion Lite." I think that's a little harsh, but it also rings true. And it hits me that every religious service I have attended since leaving the church of Christ has been an opportunity for me to critique the liturgy, the order of worship, the singing, the preaching, the prayers, to hold them up to my own church—the church I have, oddly, rejected—and still find them wanting. How sick is that? My brother is doing the same, both of us from our fundamentalist throne. No one can measure up, no one can possibly adhere to the Scriptures as we did, and although it is arrogant, I realize that if we wanted to throw down and hold an impromptu Bible Bowl, he and I could beat any two of these people—clergy included—hands down. We know our Bible and we know our God, and still, this gathering remains foreign to us. Yet I'm trying to sing along with the songs, which promise acceptance and friendship from a Jesus who loves you. Husbands reach over and rub the backs of wives. Grandparents gather grandchildren to them, and they all lift their voices in song to a benevolent God who is smiling down on them in southwest Missouri.

The treacly sweet love of God coats everything here like cotton candy, and I hate myself for thinking that way. I hate, too, that these particular Christians don't believe in four-part harmony. I am not crazy about the clapping (there's a lot) and a man down in front raises his hands over his head and begins to sway with the music. Clapping I can manage, but I can't imagine myself ever swaying. That would be too close to dancing.

I look around. The young people sit, as did we, in clusters, and they, too, carry their Bibles in those special purse-like gender-specific containers. My sweet nephew, who wants one day to grow up and be a minister, is quietly teasing a girl sitting near him. "Oh, snap!" he chortles softly, but I hear him anyway.

This is an alternate universe, and the thing that is killing me is that so many of these casually dressed people seem so sure of themselves and their faith and their God. They look happy. They pop out of their cars and squeal when they see friends, and rush across the parking lot to embrace one another as if they haven't just seen each other the night before at marriage building/Bible study/prayer group. They have this giddy joy about them that I don't recognize, and as soon as I realize that, I feel like a bat in a butterfly box. Like a tongue goes to a sore tooth, I can't stop worrying the thought. I know I am mean and judgmental, but this religion doesn't seem real to me if they all feel so damn happy about it. I don't feel that happiness. My God is not smiling. My God is pissed.

Ah, Christ, I'm going to cry during yet another song service, only I'm not crying because I'm moved by the possibility and the unrealized potential of my own faith. I'm crying because it's hopeless—isn't it?—to regain something you never had. My brother leans in again and says something that makes me sit down, fast:

"Fundamentalism broke off in us, didn't it?" he says, never taking his eyes off of the song leader.

Yes, it did. Like a sword, fundamentalism was plunged into our bodies, and then it got broken off in us so that we will never, ever heal from the wound. Like Perpetual Jesus on the Perpetual Cross, we are the walking wounded. By now, the shaft is part of our organs and these smiling, happy people? They have no idea.

And yet I know I could have been a part of this church. We are cousins, maybe even siblings. While the various congregations around New England were hoisting steeples over town greens, the seeds of discontent that would grow into my own church were being planted. But we're all believers, aren't we? It doesn't really matter, does it?

Because my people feared modernity more than Satan, they retreated from the notion of communal care. We saw poverty as a failure of the individual—and the fulfillment of God's law. Things would get worse before they got better. (Wars, rumors of wars, nation against nation, kingdom against kingdom, famines, earthquakes—all the beginning of the birth pangs.[10])

I am, however, paying attention to what looks like a budding movement within American Protestantism, something I've noticed since the lackadaisical reaction of our government after Hurricane Katrina. After that biblical devastation, politics stymied everything. Official help was late or it never came at all. People stood stranded on their roofs far longer than they should have—literally and figuratively. The winds ripped the roofs off the houses of the most impoverished families, and gave the rest of us a view into what we are overlooking in those discussions about stem-cell research and gay marriage. Even now, we still don't know how many people died in the storm and its aftermath.

When the government was nowhere to be found, church folk from around North America—believers armed with ladders and

10. Matthew 24:6–8.

hammers—stepped up. Other faith-based groups have done sig-nificant work rebuilding the Gulf Coast, but in the largest branch (Protestant) of the country's largest religious group (Christian), such a shift is cataclysmic. If this was a social gospel movement, a return to the hands-on theology rejected by my church and other fundamentalists as being too earth-bound, then I'm in.

Russell E. Richey, dean of Emory University's Candler School of Theology, thinks it may be. He remarked when I interviewed him in October 2006 that Christians' reaction to Katrina "looks more like the old social gospel." Beyond Habitat for Humanity, a Georgia- and faith-based group, the faithfulness of common, everyday church folks in Katrina's wake is a story repeated up and down the Gulf Coast. The Mississippi chapter of the Na-tional Association for the Advancement of Colored People stated that support has come from such groups as the Southern Bap-tists, Methodists, Roman Catholics, and the National Council of Churches, which has organized congregations to help rebuild African American congregations in New Orleans. An NAACP report on rebuilding Mississippi concluded that even a year after Katrina, faith groups continued to be the most effective respon-ders to the crisis, though few of them had received assistance, compensation, or training in disaster relief. If you talk to people in Gulfport, Mississippi, as I did in 2006, what you'll hear is that without church folks, that town and others like it wouldn't have survived. Gulfport is still a long way from being back to where it needs to be, but it's a lot farther along than it would have been without the believers.

It's a common phenomenon that people respond in times of crisis. Look at the outpouring of donations after the 2004 tsunami in the Indian Ocean. But this may go deeper. Nationally, there is evidence that church groups have widened their focus beyond dis-asters, to issues including the protection of the environment, the halt of the genocide in the Darfur region of Sudan, and opposition to the Iraq war. The World Council of Churches met in early 2006 and denounced the Iraq war—and went the extra step of apologizing to the world for the loss inflicted because of that war. The U.S. conference of the council went further and said in a statement: "Hurricane Katrina revealed to the world those left behind in our own nation by the rupture of our social contract. As a nation we have refused to confront the racism that infects our policies around the world."

Rick Warren, the Baptist pastor of the California-based Saddleback Church and author of the Purpose-Driven Life series, includes poverty, illiteracy, and disease as issues that need the attention of the faithful. His goal, he says, is "a second Reformation."[11]

In 2006, Robert W. Edgar, general secretary of the National Council of Churches USA, published *Middle Church: Reclaiming the Moral Values of the Faithful Majority from the Religious Right*. He was in the midst of writing it, he told me in a 2006 interview, when the deadly Indian Ocean tsunami hit in December 2004. His book joins a shelf full of other new books, including one by former U.S. senator John Danforth, *Faith and Politics: How the "Moral Values" Debate Divides America and How to Move Foward*, that call upon believers to focus more on social action and less on discussions about esoteric topics that don't get the hungry fed. Even Warren, who opposes stem-cell research, has thrown his considerable weight behind social initiatives, including World AIDS Day. Appearing on *The Daily Show with Jon Stewart* in December 2006, Danforth, an Episcopalian priest (from Missouri!) and former ambassador to the United Nations, said politicians choose to blur the line between their jobs and religion in order to energize the voter base. In fact, he said, religion has been used of late to divide people. It's good political strategy to focus on stem-

---

11. The first Reformation, as we all know, being a movement in the sixteenth century, popularly thought to have started with Martin Luther but begun earlier with the works of John Wycliffe and others.

cell research and abortion—and sidestep entirely the needs of the poor. Responding to a newspaper column in the late '70s about the refugee crisis in Cambodia, then-senator Danforth flew to Cambodia. "The lesson I learned is the difference between agenda and concern," he writes. "Had we been intent on a fixed agenda ... we would have failed, however desirable the agenda was ... Concern rather than an agenda appealed to the conscience of the world."

This is not to say that all Christian groups are quite ready for the switch. In 2006, the wheezing old Christian Coalition lost its president-elect, Joel Hunter, over the Coalition's inability to, as reported in *Time* magazine and other media, rise above the belt and stop focusing on abortion and homosexuality and start looking at larger world issues. Hunter departed when the Coalition decided that his services were not needed. Those services would have included, according to the press release issued at the time of his appointment, "the care of creation, helping society's marginalized, human rights/religious issues and compassion issues." It was gutsy of the Coalition to appoint as its leader a critic of the Christian Right, but the organization just couldn't follow through.

According to Hunter, those compassion issues include poverty, justice, and caring for the environment. (Those same issues, according to a study by the University of Michigan and the University of Texas, drove the gender gap during the 2000 presidential election. In short, women tend to vote more as liberals with respect to social justice issues. Maybe we just listen better.)

But that's the Christian Coalition, whose members don't appear to understand that needs and desires (and politics) change. Other, more moderate Christians sense that something's changing. Robert Hodgson Jr., dean of the American Bible Society's Nida Institute for Biblical Scholarship, said, when I interviewed him in October 2006, that forays into the social gospel—or something like it—can be considered course corrections to "perhaps overly individualistic readings of the Scripture. I think if you scratch any of our faith traditions, you will find that there are both spiritual and corporal concerns."

What if the pendulum of American Protestantism is swinging back, away from the self-involved, self-absorbed concern for one's own salvation, and toward the temporal well-being of others? What if we are at the beginning of a modern-day social gospel movement, the same kind of movement that pushed forward the Salvation Army and the Boy Scouts and the YMCA? What if we stopped arguing about hot-button social issues and started feeding the hungry, clothing the naked, and housing the homeless? The phrase these days is "red-letter Christian," meaning those believers who concentrate specifically on the words spoken by Jesus. Those words are, in the Bible, often printed in red. The phrase has been given some circulation by Tony Campolo, a noted progressive evangelical, in his essays on the religion and spirituality website beliefnet.com, and in his books, including *Letters to a Young Evangelical: The Art of Mentoring.*[12]

It's a crazy thought, but what if we became red-letter Christians, concentrating specifically on the words that Jesus spoke? What if we took the advice of Jay Bakker, the skater/punk/tattooed pastor and son of Jim and Tammy Faye, and paid attention not to the arguments of the day but to the exhortation to love one another, without any particular agenda? What if we just agree to disagree, as Bakker suggests, and move on to the topics at hand, the kinds of things that seemed to get Jesus's attention—hunger, poverty, hopelessness, equality, fairness? What if we put our energies into making the world better, and let the rest of the agenda fall by the wayside, where it so rightfully belongs? I speak for the believers in whom, as my brother said, the church broke off into. We were thrust through with the sword of faith, and then it broke

12. Interestingly, the phrase "red-letter Christian" is said to have been coined by a Jewish country and western DJ, in an interview with progressive Christian Jim Wallis.

off in us, and we cannot pull it out and we cannot be free of the discomfort of its presence. We want healing and we want an active faith. We want a return to the early church, where people shared, where the point was not acquisition of material goods, but making sure that you were walking with God and that your neighbor had food and clothes. We have strayed so far afield that for some of us, the way back seems impossibly hard. We need to return to the original intent of our religion. We are dying for that. When I was young and sang "A Beautiful Life," with its promise to do a good deed every day, I took those words literally. Every day, I would do something kind for someone, and not because I would be rewarded for it, but because God desired that it be done, because it was the right thing to do. "My life on earth is but a span, and so I'll do the best I can (the best I can)." Sing it, basses!

Am I angry here in the stands of this smallish megachurch because they know something I don't? Have they decided to go back to that earlier faith, the one I yearn for?

Because, if we do that? I'm in. I'm *so* in. Until then, though, I will yearn for a faith I know is out there, somewhere.

Ten

WATER JUGS

Bear with me a moment, but this has been a long time coming. Say you're a young and impressionable girl. You don't understand a good 70 percent of what's going on around you in the adult world from which you can't escape, but one day, a nice man (or woman) offers you a solid ledge on which to stand, where you will be protected by a Supreme Being who will neither leave you nor hurt you by staying.

Say you want to fiercely love that Being, because you're told you're supposed to and because it feels right, but say the ledge is a short distance from where you're standing, and say, on the walk, you get sidetracked into believing that your love—and you, come to think of it—aren't quite what the Supreme Being (or his Son, Jesus) had in mind. Say you keep walking even though the way gets darker and you get scared and angry at the same time, because no matter what you do, you can never measure up to either the journey or the Being, because you're a girl.

What do you do? How do you feel about that? There's the solid ledge just over there, but on the journey to it, you discover that it's out of your reach anyway. And even though you're a little girl, you know you are capable of great acts of courage and large acts of love. Say the message you're getting is that all those things don't matter, because you won't measure up.

What do you do? You might give up for a while because, really, what's the point?

But then you decide to backtrack, return to the beginning of the path, and see if maybe you've stepped off the proper trail and wandered off somewhere bad, somewhere hurtful. It happens. Because, on paper? The path and the Supreme Being and the Supreme Being's offspring make perfect sense to you. You suspect you could at least be a contributing member here.

And then you remember a story:

At noon one day near the Samarian city of Sychar, a native woman came to a well that was historically significant to the Jews, the well of the patriarch Jacob.[1] Near here, Jacob had willed a large portion of his land to his favored son, Joseph, ancestor of Jesus.[2] The Samaritan woman came to the well for water, and was surprised when a Jew waiting there asked her for a drink. Jews of that time were notorious for their prejudice against Samaritans, yet here was a Jewish man asking to drink from a Samaritan water jug—a fairly intimate act that implied trust on the part of the drinker. Who, after all, knew where the jug had been? And add to that the fact that the jug was carried by a Samaritan—a Samaritan woman, no less. None of this would have made the water at all attractive to the Jew asking for it. In fact, that the Jew had even shown his face in Samaria was unusual. Devout Jews made a point of going the long way around the region to avoid meeting Samaritans.[3]

1. John 4:4–42.
2. Genesis 48:22.
3. The historical reason behind the schism is complicated, but boiled down, Jews of that time did not think Samaritans were Jewish enough, in part because they'd mixed Jewish law with pagan practices, and they'd intermarried with non-Jews.

What followed was a frank discussion between the Jew—Jesus—and the woman, who remains nameless in the fourth chapter of John, and is overlooked entirely in the Gospels of Matthew, Mark, and Luke.[4]

It becomes obvious rather early in the story that Jesus had no intention of avoiding an encounter with either a Samaritan or a woman. He had been resting at the well while his disciples went into the village to search for food. In their short but lively discussion, Jesus tells the woman an allegorical story about water that will forever quench thirst—"living water." He is speaking of the gift of eternal life, but this is not the kind of conversation one would expect at a well on any given day, and so the woman takes him literally.[5] Interrupted in her duties, she does not understand. She is both skeptical and intrigued. Show me this water, she says, so I don't have to fetch water ever again. As they continue to talk, Jesus says that he knows that the woman, who has been married five times, is now living with a man to whom she is not married. This piques the woman's interest even more. Who is this man who can tell intimate details about her after just one meeting? Could this be the Messiah, perhaps? But that can't be. She is a Samaritan, hardly worthy of attention from a Jew, much less the promised Messiah. And so, to push that thought from her head, maybe, she admits to Jesus that she doesn't even worship where pious Jews tell her to worship—in Jerusalem, at the temple. Jesus assures her that she is not wrong to worship in the nearby mountains—perhaps on Mount Gerizim, later the site of a Samaritan temple—rather than Jerusalem.[6] Worrying about the site of wor-

---

4. You can make a whole study of the people, places, and things left out of the various Gospels. In fact, people have.

5. And who hasn't made the mistake of taking an allegory as the literal word?

6. In fact, the place of worship was a very big deal for both Jews and Samaritans. Generations earlier, the Samaritans had formed their own version of Judaism based on the Torah.

ship is hardly important to Jesus. He is, after all, creating a new kingdom, like the water he mentioned earlier, that is not of the world, in which what used to be considered significant religious sites won't matter. The woman—maybe seeking to appear religious to this stranger, after all—mentions that she is waiting for a messiah, and Jesus identifies himself as the one for whom she is waiting.

At this point, the disciples return. They are "astonished," according to John 4:27, to see Jesus talking with an unaccompanied woman, but they say nothing. This is not always the case. In other situations where Jesus is found talking to someone his disciples consider beneath him—and this is usually the reaction of his followers, who haven't quite grasped the radical message he is sharing—they have been quick to correct him.[7] This time, though, they watch as the woman leaves her water jug and goes into Sychar to tell the townspeople that she may have met the Christ. The townspeople follow her out to Jesus and ask him to stay, which he does, for two days. Many Samaritans come to believe in him in that time, and they tell the woman that they came to their beliefs on their own, and not because of anything she'd said to them about Jesus's ability to tell someone's past. That certainly puts the unnamed woman in her place. She shouldn't think that she, a mere woman, has influenced their decisions.

But I kind of think she did. If she hadn't left the well and spread the news, who's to say the townspeople would have ever heard Jesus's message?

Throughout history, says feminist theologian Elisabeth Moltmann-Wendel, water jugs have been a symbol associated with women. Women of significance in the Bible are often portrayed

---

7. In Luke 7:36–50, when Simon the Pharisee has Jesus over for a meal, a local woman comes and washes Jesus's feet with her tears and anoints him with perfume, and Simon sits and thinks to himself that if Jesus really were a prophet, he'd know this woman was a bad woman, but Jesus sets him straight.

either holding a water jug or container or in close proximity to one. Abraham straps a water container onto Hagar's shoulder before he sends her wandering with her son in Genesis 21:14. Rebekah lets Abraham's servant drink from her jar in Genesis 24, and opens up a whole can of worms with Isaac. You get the idea. You see a woman, and a water container is most likely somewhere nearby.

In light of the importance of women and water and wells and fetching water from those wells, that the Samaritan woman leaves her jug at the well to go alert the town is significant. The news she wants to share must have seemed important. Jesus tells her things she hasn't heard before. He is not on earth to repeat the messages women of her day were accustomed to hearing—which were certainly not messages extolling their worth and valuing their souls as equal to those of men. The messages women were receiving did not make them candidates to abandon their daily work—gathering water, in this case—to follow a religious teacher. According to the culture of the time, Jesus wasn't even supposed to be talking to her, a lone woman, and a lowly Samaritan.

His doing so is yet another inspired shift in the world that up to then would have discouraged a discussion between a man and a woman at a well, whatever their cultural backgrounds. But Jesus was on earth to change precisely everything, from the way farmers plowed their fields to the way women moved through society. And it was a message that was well received, at least by the women who are recorded in the Bible. A core group of women of his day responded quickly to his message of equality, as reiterated years later in Paul's letter to the Galatians: "There is no longer Jew nor Greek, there is no longer slave or free, there is no longer male and female; for all of you are one in Christ Jesus."[8]

I don't remember reading that particular verse as a girl. Oh, I am sure I did, and I am sure I thought that it pertained to slaves

8. Galatians 3:28.

171

and free people, as an indication that Abraham Lincoln had it right all along. Because the freeing of the slaves—at least on paper—was an accomplished fact, I would not have looked to the rest of the verse as anything applicable to me or my life. I read the verse as I read other verses. I simply embraced it with the rest of the Scriptures as a nice-enough sentiment but not one that would tilt my world. Of course there were still Jews and Greeks, and males and females. The only significant barrier we'd crossed, to my knowledge, was blurring the line between slave and free. So the Bible and Abraham Lincoln were both right on this count.[9]

All this time, the answer was staring me in the face. I had only to listen.

I remember sitting in Sunday school getting increasingly agitated at the Jews of Moses' time, and at the Jews of Jesus's time. Couldn't they see the significance of the message they were hearing? Why did they continually have to be told again, and shown miracles, in order to get the point that was clear even to me, an eight-year-old?

Hmm.

So how did the women of Jesus's day view him? I imagine if we knew this, we could cut through a great deal of the nonsense we face now, the same mentality that bars women from roles as leaders in the churches. In a confession that was every bit as powerful as Peter's in the early days of Jesus's ministry, Martha recognized Jesus as "the Christ."[10] She enjoyed a relationship that allowed

9. But, to be honest? I can't say that my history education was all that detailed. What children of the northern states learned to call the Civil War we were taught to call the War Between the States. My friends just over the border in Arkansas learned that it was more accurately known as the War of Northern Aggression. My friends lived just ninety miles away, near Pea Ridge and the battlefield there. That same sentiment bled into Missouri. We were in the thick of it just a little over a century beforehand, but you wouldn't have known it from our textbooks.

10. John 11:27 (Martha's) and Mark 8:29 (Peter's).

both disagreement and mutual respect, as found in Luke 10:41, when Jesus reminded her that she was worrying too much about worldly things. Jesus had come to her house, and she had reacted in a flurry of preparations, and resented that her sister, Mary, had instead sat at Jesus's feet to hear his message. When she asked Jesus to tell Mary to get up and help, he told her that her sister was paying attention to the important matters, while Martha was missing the whole spiritual point. Abandon your role for a moment, he said, and listen. Put down the water jug.

Yet in other circumstances, Martha could also be bold—chastising Jesus for not arriving at her home in time to save her dying brother, Lazarus—and she could be forthright by running out into the road to meet him to deliver that chastisement.[11]

From all indications, Joanna, the wife of Herod's steward Chuza, a woman who'd earlier been healed by Jesus, actually left the palace to follow him.[12] This would have been unheard of prior to Jesus's radical message. What Jesus was doing, according to Andrew Greeley, writing in *Jesus: A Meditation on His Stories and His Relationships with Women,* "was simply not done." The women of Herod's regime, while not elevated to the same cultural level as the men, were certainly privy to a life that was opulent compared to the Jewish woman on the street—say, that of Martha. Leaving home to follow a man like Jesus would have been unthinkable. Still, something in the message spoke to her, and Joanna was moved to abandon—or at least place in jeopardy—her relatively privileged life. Herod's father, after all, had tried to kill the infant Jesus. Surely there was some familial animosity in Herod's court over the Messiah who got away.

The historically maligned Mary Magdalene followed Jesus to the grave,[13] even while his male disciples abandoned him in his

---

11. John 11:20–21.
12. Luke 8:3.
13. Matthew 27:55–56.

worst hour. She was known as "the sweet friend of God." In public discussion shaken loose by Dan Brown's enormously popular novel *The Da Vinci Code,* Mary Magdalene only partly gained back her reputation. Centuries after exegetical distortion moved this pious woman into the realm of whoredom, she is still depicted as perhaps too close to Jesus, physically. Did they marry? Did they have sex? Does it matter? Can't we look to Mary Magdalene as simply an early church leader whose rightful place next to Christ should have been acknowledged? There are no Scriptures to place her anywhere but right next to Jesus. Even a cursory reading of the Bible shows her to be a godly woman responding wholeheartedly to a message that must have appealed to her greatly. But the fastest way to rob a woman of her power is to make her a sexual suspect. It certainly has worked all these years for MM.

Of course, each woman would have an individual response to Jesus, but judging from what we know of their surroundings, many women certainly had a positive one. Scattered throughout the Gospels are stories similar to that of the jug-bearing Samaritan woman, where the female object of Jesus's attention is at first incredulous, then surprised, then excited to be addressed as an equal by such a compassionate and obviously learned man.[14] Invariably, the stories end with the woman returning to her place of origin to share the message with her counterparts—as with the healing of Jairus's daughter in Matthew 9:18–26, when "the report of this spread throughout the district." In that healing as in so many others involving women, Jesus intentionally highlighted their plight, and as tempting as it might be to label it so, this is not simply a feminist retelling. Jesus showed special attention to women at a time when such attention must have been like water—everlasting or garden variety, it doesn't matter—on a dry tongue. In the book of Luke, a woman crippled for eighteen long

14. The common conclusion appears to have been: "He knows me. He *really* knows me!"

years—bent over and unable to stand—comes to Jesus, and he places his hands on her and calls her a "daughter of Abraham."[15] Critics in the crowd—and there were always critics in the crowd —worry that Jesus performed this healing on the Sabbath, and he reminds him that the law allows them to tend to their animals on the Sabbath, yet they would have a woman remain bent over because of the misinterpretation of a religious law? "You hypocrites," he says. No one asked for the miracle—including the woman—yet Jesus heals her so she can stand upright, and then welcomes her into the fold by calling her "daughter."

Besides the obvious benefits of physical healing, how much of the good news that the women seemed so anxious to share centered on their acceptance as disciples on a par with Jesus's male followers? The hope of eternal life seems to so many to be confusing, at least at first. What kind of water is living?

Maybe Jesus's women are, instead, reacting positively to a spiritual leader who is talking to them face-to-face and giving them access to knowledge that up to then they had not possessed.

It should be noted here that the most celebrated of New Testament women, Mary, Jesus's mother, had quite a different response to his ministry. She feared for his safety, a fitting reaction for any mother worth her salt. Perhaps Mary was acting here not as the mother of God, but the mother of the man, Jesus. Then, too, it is hard to gauge a man's influence on the world through his mother's reaction to him. Mary the mother of Jesus gives us a view into his humanity, for Jesus was quite human. In regard to familial loyalty and the like, Jesus set an example when he chose his own family in Mark 3:31–35. His mother and brothers, he said, were the people who followed him.

Outside of his biological family, when women called him "Savior," they may have been speaking of the temporal as well as the spiritual world. Jesus came and patterned for everyone a

15. Luke 13:16.

world of equals. Maybe that is how women who followed Jesus saw him, as a savior, and not just in the spiritual realm. Here was a man who was preaching and teaching and living a life of equality in a world of sharply defined gender roles. Here was a man who insisted on conversation with people whom society had rendered invisible—the women, the sick, the poor. How much more powerful was his message when he spoke to a poor, sick woman? Here was a man who was willing to do more than just talk with women, an attitude that was striking when compared to how the rest of the male world saw their female counterparts, writes Graham N. Stanton in *The Gospels and Jesus*. By contrast, Jesus moved naturally among the "tribe of women."

In order to understand just how radical was Jesus's message, it is necessary to understand the ancient world in which it was first delivered. During Jesus's time, the Mediterranean culture was measured by bureaucracy, class, and honor, as related mostly to the distribution of wealth. A gender-based honor-and-shame moral system defined the culture, with the bulk of the shame residing in the feminine world. In the ancient Jewish world (surely this sounds familiar to people outside the Jewish world, too), women were held in lower esteem than men, as they'd been assigned the role of originator of sin.

As a member of the originating class, I have never been entirely comfortable laying on Eve's thin shoulders the entire blame for bringing sin into the garden. Who's to say what God's plan was for sin, anyway?

For those of us who take our religion straight, she is our First Woman. Not coincidentally, she was also our First Woman Who Attempted to Have It All. The second role often follows the first. First, there is Woman. Then, there is Woman Doing Everything. And so it has always been.

That, I think we can blame on Eve, that she tried to chew that fruit of the tree of knowledge of good and evil with her mouth open, but not for reasons we may think. In the beginning, the

First Woman and her companion, Adam, flitted through paradise. They pulled fruit off the trees and ate it. They didn't appear to have any responsibilities. They certainly didn't work. It was one long continuous vacation in Florida, before the invasion of theme parks. Then a serpent persuaded Eve to eat from the tree in the middle of the garden, the only one God had said to steer clear of, or risk death.[16]

But Eve ate after the serpent reassured her that she wouldn't die. Instead, she'd be smart, like God. The prospect was so tempting that Eve not only ate, she offered the forbidden fruit to Adam. After their snack, the two realized they were naked, so they made clothing from fig leaves and tried to remember what life was like back when they were ignorant and happy.[17]

The punishment came later, when God, the Cosmic Parent, discovered their crime. And so God handed out retribution: The serpent was cursed to crawl on its belly for eternity and suffer the hatred of humans. Adam would have to work for his meals. And, oh, yes! Eventually he would die. But God hit Eve where it hurt. Because of her role in the whole mess, Eve and her daughters would forevermore suffer pain in childbirth. She would also labor under a new desire for her husband, and if she pursued that desire at the risk of turning away from God, she would be dominated by her mate.

See what happens when a woman wants to have it all? All hell

---

16. Anecdotally, the forbidden fruit eventually came to be identified with the apple, although there is no scriptural reference that the fruit was so named, just as there is no Old Testament reference that the creature that swallowed Jonah was a whale. The Bible refers to it only as a "big fish" in the book of Jonah. In some translations, including my New American Standard Version, the creature in Jonah's story is referred to as a "sea monster" (Matt. 12:40).

17. Much has been made of how Adam and Eve, upon realizing that they were naked, immediately sought to clothe themselves. But I learned to change into my swimsuit underneath a towel at Green Valley Bible Camp. I know modesty when I see it.

breaks loose, and the rest of us pay for it forever. Sitting through countless sessions in Sunday school, I arrived at the notion independent of the teachers I had that history hadn't been especially kind or even fair to Eve. We were taught to feel for her a kind of enmity, but I thought she was only doing what any right-minded woman would do. She sought wisdom. Still, the curse continues. Women who attempt the seemingly impossible feat of possessing a happy and loving partnership; happy children, if they choose to have them; and, these days, employment that feeds their souls, risk bringing down the wrath of God.

Or the latest political curse, whichever is most handy.

It's not just Eve's comeuppance chasing us back to ignorance. Our popular culture repeats the message over and over, even while those odd examples of the successful woman are held in front of us like a carrot—or an apple—on a string.

Author Carla Ricci paints a stark picture of women in ancient Mediterranean society. According to Ricci, a woman's social position was on the same level as that of children and slaves. In such a segregated society, woman's fortune was entirely tied to that of her husband. Boys went to school—girls didn't—which only perpetuated a system that limited women to hearth and home.

However, there is a growing body of literature that suggests the first-century Jewish world inhabited by Jesus and his followers was "more nuanced" in its approach to independent women. Most of what we believe to be true about first-century Judaism in fact comes from rabbinical writings, such as the Talmud, which weren't transcribed until some centuries after the life of Jesus. We have scant few accounts from women of the time. But Mosaic law contained some fairly restrictive rules in regard to women, in particular in regard to their menstruation. If the original law was devoted more to cleanliness and health—as were dietary laws—than to the cultural restriction of women, there is some thought that this law was reinforced by bodies of writing such as the Mishnah, the first recording of the Oral Torah, in part to quell the growing equality fostered by early Christianity. In other words, the older law was in place in no small part to help ensure the physical safety of the Jews. As early Christianity and its message of oneness between the genders gained a toehold and then a foothold in ancient Mediterranean society, subsequent Jewish writings came down harder on restricting the movement and lives of females, which was hardly the laws' original intent.

Even if the original law had been more egalitarian, Jesus frequently flew in the face of it, both in practices of worship, and in his approach to women. In Luke 8:43–48, Jesus shattered an age-old restriction against touching a woman who had been bleeding (for twelve years!) by allowing her to touch him and—again—welcoming her into the fold by calling her "daughter."

It must be noted, too, that Jews of Jesus's time lived and labored under Roman rule, which would have had an obvious effect on Jewish society's rules and mores in regard to equality between the genders, perhaps a loosening of the boundaries embraced by the Judaic society. Yet the actual effect of Roman rule on women's roles in Judaic society is something else we don't know with certainty, nor can we guess as to how that rule played itself out in the naturally occurring tension between the Jewish sects, a struggle that also would have had some effect on the plight of women. We do not have the original text, and we must take much of what we believe on faithful speculation (which, for a fundamentalist, is a scary word). As Miriam Therese Winter writes in *The Chronicle of Noah and Her Sisters*, "If Sarah had kept a diary, we would have had to speculate less."

But we can at least make some reasoned guesses. In ancient Palestine, the public realm belonged to men. Most of women's activities were confined to the home. For the most part, only women of a lower class (in a society with a nearly nonexistent middle class) left the home to work. The home was the exclusive domain of the woman.

Yet Jesus did not seem responsive to the gender-based cultural pressures of his day, and outside of a divine imperative for his behaving so, we can only speculate as to why. In regard to Jesus's own human context, his lineage contained sexually suspect women, including Tamar, Rahab, and Bathsheba, according to Ann Belford Ulanov in *The Female Ancestors of Christ*.[18] There is every reason to believe Jesus knew his own lineage, and perhaps this knowledge gave him some insight into forgiveness and personal responsibility. Was Jesus responsible for the actions of these female ancestors? Should their sexual sins have been laid at his feet? If the answer is no—and Jesus gave every indication that it was—then why would the women of Jesus's day continue to carry the traditional societal burden of Eve's sin?[19]

In fact, the life of Jesus is a perfect example of just how artificial were and are gender stereotypes. He simply did not recognize them, perhaps because from what we know about him, he'd already integrated behavior characteristics attributed to both genders. What theologian Elisabeth Schüssler Fiorenza called Jesus's "inclusive graciousness" is played out again and again in his parables and in his dealings with women. In Mark 7:24–30, Jesus backed away from calling Gentiles "dogs" when a woman whose daughter was possessed by a demon entreated him to help her. When Jesus likened his message to food that must go to the children first, and then perhaps later to the dogs, the woman answered quickly, "Sir, even the dogs under the table eat the children's crumbs." Jesus was so impressed by the answer—which was, one suspects, one he'd hoped to hear to help spread his message—that he healed the woman's daughter sight unseen. So he is

18. In order, that meant Jesus was related by blood to someone who posed as a temple prostitute (and became pregnant by her father-in-law), a prostitute-spy, and a woman who slept with King David and later had her husband killed in battle so that David could have her to himself. Man, but I wish I could have lived in Old Testament times!

19. And besides: the sins die with the sinner (Ezek. 18:20).

a man willing to listen to the reason of a woman. He is a man who is willing to back away from his earlier statements, correct them, and in this instance do the right thing in regard to a woman and her daughter.[20]

Another radical departure taken by Jesus was that he approached women as people and not as temptresses. Never once is it recorded that Jesus reminded a woman—as Jewish law did —that she was the daughter of Eve, nor did he hint that women were responsible for any sin other than their own. It simply was not an issue for him, and that must have been a freeing thing for women of that time to hear. It was one more radical approach for this rebel rabbi, and one that had to have been—excuse my speculation but I doubt I'm going out on a limb—intoxicating to women.

Indications are that the first Christians took Jesus's egalitarian teaching to heart. Wealthy women—again, then as now, wealth was one of the main determining factors of a person's influence —had decisive influence over Christian gatherings, according to Fiorenza. In Philippians 4:2, the writer urges two obviously influential women to settle their differences. In Romans 16:1, Phoebe is named a female deacon.[21]

Historians say that women may have been prominent in the early church even into the second century. The writer of Colossians sends greetings to Nympha and the church in her house.[22]

But the egalitarian attitude toward women that Jesus practiced did not last among his followers much past his short life. Patriarchy reasserted itself—gradually, but decisively. There are

20. And as such, might I add, he is the perfect boyfriend.

21. This is yet another verse my Sunday school teachers slid right past. When I asked, they told me that "deacon" meant something different, more like "Sunday school teacher" in the early church. I suppose it also meant "Sunday school teacher but only until the young men in class reach age twelve."

22. Colossians 4:15.

a number of explanations for this—and far too many to explore here. Many subsequent male scribes responsible for recording the Bible were culturally attuned to the experience of Jesus's male followers, perceiving the theological and missionary role of women as "profoundly unsettling" to male disciples, who saw themselves as "privileged associates" of Jesus, even though Jesus seems to have "gotten along quite well without them," according to Sandra M. Schneiders in her *The Revelation Text: Interpreting the New Testament as Sacred Scriptures*. It would appear that the writer of the fourth Gospel, at least, was aware of the tension that women in leadership roles aroused in the community, and wanted, writes Schneiders, to "present Jesus as legitimating female participation in male-appropriated roles." But the message is ignored or rewritten to seem minor in Jesus's teachings—an afterthought, really.

But if Jesus had been parroting the patriarchal message women had been hearing all along in his day, chances are he would not have enjoyed such an easy relationship with them. They would not have felt so comfortable talking to him, running out into the road to greet him, allowing him to lay hands on them to heal them.

In the same vein, the traditional patriarchal Christian message—not Jesus's original message, but the one we hear today—has had a chilling effect on today's church. In reaction to the boys-only club of some churches (including the church of my youth), women have thrown up their hands and gone far afield from Christianity in search of an alternative approach.

Do you blame us?

In fact, writer after writer uses the Bible as the key tool against women's emancipation. With no thought to context, certain members of today's churches repeat the (misinterpreted) canard that women are to keep silent in the assembly, and that women are not to usurp authority over a man. Those same elect point to commonly held historical interpretations of the sacred text that wrongly insist there were no female apostles or early church leaders. The role of women has been deleted or greatly discounted in subsequent retellings of the biblical stories, and for some Christians, this renders revisiting the Scriptures problematic at best. If the text is called divine, or divinely inspired, there is little room for interpretation—and far too much trust placed in the hands of unseen and unknown authors from long ago. The same rigorous scrutiny one would bring to, say, a new insurance policy is not practiced in regard to the Bible.[23]

Only by looking at the data as a whole can we come to understand Jesus and his honest and historical approach to gender. And then perhaps we, too, can respond as Martha did, with a resounding and matter-of-fact confession that Jesus is the Christ, and his message applies equally to all of us. Only then can we put down our water jugs and follow freely.

Until then, I am stuck.

In the years after I left the church of Christ, if someone asked if I was a Christian, I would say no. I knew Christians at my old church—real, live, Bible-breathing Christians—and I certainly didn't measure up. It wasn't a matter of denying Christ. It was a matter of honestly assessing my worth.

And then I amended that answer to say that I was certainly trying. That seemed to appease people who then didn't feel nearly the same motivation to save me.

Then I started saying I'm a floater. That always required an explanation. I float between faiths, but yeah, generally I stay in the realm of Christianity.

23. In fact, according to Stephen Prothero, author of the 2007 book *Religious Literacy: What Every American Needs to Know—And Doesn't*, most Americans can't even name the first book of the Bible (Genesis, silly), much less quote Scriptures accurately. Strange that we cling to a book we don't bother to read.

Ironically, as in my heart I walked back to the origin of my faith, my answers got increasingly tepid. And we know what happens to tepid Christians.[24]

And then came the day when I realized that I had for most of my adult life, since I left the church of my girlhood in my early thirties, let others define my faith for me. Don't go to church three times a week? Then you can't call yourself a Christian. Don't believe in the tenets of the church of Christ? Then you can't call yourself a Christian. Don't bend your knee in fear at a thunderstorm, anxious that perhaps this is Jesus's dreaded and hoped-for return on earth, where he will hold up a yardstick to all of us, and you haven't a chance, you selfish sinner, of measuring up? Then don't call yourself a Christian. You don't deserve it.

Everyone has their interior voices. Mine are often male, and they belong to (I assume) well-meaning men from my old church. The women didn't figure much, but the men are quick to explain my place in the firmament. And after a while I just didn't have it in me anymore to argue. I let others define me and felt comfortable about it.

Shame on me.

If I'd been paying attention to Jesus's message in the first place, none of those harmful Sunday school lessons or girls'-only Bible classes would have made a dent in my faith. I would have stood up and said, "This is wrong," and either saved everyone an uncomfortable hour or so and gotten a ride home, or stood there and talked about Jesus's real message.

Years after I left my last church of Christ—a smallish congregation in my new hometown in Connecticut—I met a woman I'd sat by at Sunday school when I was still a member. I was excited to see her. I remembered her as being smart and funny and found that she, too, had left the church. She'd found another church home in a denomination that in no way resembled our old church,

---

24. They get spat out of Jesus's mouth (Rev. 3:16.)

but she didn't try to proselytize, which I appreciated. We talked about the Sunday school classes we'd shared as adults in that little church, and she reminded me that even then I had argued—out loud—about women's role in the church. She said I'd never raised my voice, but had spoken forcefully about what I saw as the church's error in keeping women in the pews and out of the pulpit. It had caused some uncomfortable moments, she said. I was considered by other women in the class a legacy, she said, in that I'd been raised in the church of Christ, I wasn't a recent convert, and so it caused a stir that I was questioning what to the members' minds was the infallibility of the Bible. (The fact that I was a young divorced mother probably added to the stir, but she didn't say that; I refused to walk with my head down over the failure of my marriage. I made that marriage, I killed it, and no one got a vote.) She said she had admired my speaking up like that, and she had long wished she could tell me that she wished she'd spoken up in support of what I was saying, which made perfect sense to her at the time.

But she just couldn't.

And I don't even remember making much of an effort to argue about Jesus's egalitarian view of gender roles once I reached adulthood. If I argued at all in those long-ago Bible classes, it was—yes!—tepidly, but I imagine we both ought to go easy on ourselves. We did what we could, and then we left. I can't speak for my friend, but I can speak for myself: I leave it to others to work from the inside for change. I'm going to stand right here. As much as I miss harmonizing with my fractured alto on the hymns that scared the shit out of me, this is me standing over here by myself.

But I still love Jesus.

Eleven

JESUS HAUNTS ME,
THIS I KNOW

You want Christ-haunted?

I ask my bosses at my newspaper to send me to Port-au-Prince, Haiti, for a story. I want to go with a group of faithful folks —most of them Catholic—whose church has a mission in the country and a fondness for the people on that part of a screwed-over island. Over there, just over the *monts* (mountains), is the Dominican Republic, with its tourism and Spanish and sandy-white beaches. Over here, seeped in the tangy cocktail of diesel, charcoal, and human waste, there is *Kreyòl* and babies who weigh no more than spiders. I will follow this church group as they visit orphanages and hospitals. I will be attuned to their every conversation, their fears, and those moments at night when they are so shell-shocked by what they have seen that they won't be able to speak. I am a professional and I have seen things I don't talk about, and so I consider myself prepared for the worst Haiti has to offer. For more bolstering, I read every book I can get my hands on that explores the painful puzzle of this island of Ayiti. I read two books by Paul Farmer, a Harvard-trained doctor who has made it his life's work to heal Haiti, and I read Tracy Kidder's book about Farmer, *Mountains beyond Mountains: Healing the World*. I read three books by journalists, and *The Comedians,* a Graham Greene novel based in Haiti.

A photographer at my newspaper grew up in Haiti. We will work as a team. He loans me books, as well. In addition to his evocative portraits, the photographer is also an internationally recognized poet. So although he doesn't suggest it, I read his books too.

We arrive one hot July day on what at the time is the daily American flight to Port-au-Prince, and even though I am book-smart, I am woefully ill-prepared for the assault on my senses. I have never in my life seen such poverty, such degradation. And I know that my country has played a major role in helping destroy this country.

Over the years, the organizers of these kinds of immersion trips have developed what they believe to be a remedy for reactions such as mine. Every night on an open-air patio in a fine house—a near-mansion—where the mission is housed, they will gather everyone in folding chairs so that we can talk about our day. Everything is fair game, but it doesn't always work, and it doesn't escape the notice of some of the faithful that this house where we are staying is far, far finer than anything we've seen all day in the hot, acrid streets. The former owners of this place, a family that made millions from sugar, have gone, and the Catholic Church has stepped in. The house is high on a hill, with a gate and a guard. We are told that wandering the streets is dangerous, but I am with the photographer, a Kreyòl-speaking native, and we wander anyway. The Americans who live in this fine house do God's work here with the help of household staff that cooks and washes their clothes—by hand, in a tub out back. I know this because one day I am up on the roof and I look down into a small courtyard. We'd been encouraged to let the staff take care of our dirty clothes—and clothes in this tropical climate get very dirty, as

you sweat a lot—so one morning I bundle mine together and they
are whisked away by I-don't-know-who. Up on the roof, I happen to look down and see the women washing them in a large tub
with lots of suds. I know they are my clothes because I recognize
a striking orange dress I bought (and will leave behind) strictly for
this trip. I suppose I thought someone just tossed them into a May-
tag in the basement; I had no idea of the laborious effort getting
my clothes washed in this house would entail. I vow, even though
I pay the women handsomely, not to have my clothes washed in
Haiti again. I do not feel right, even though the exchange puts
money in the pockets of Haitians, and when I try to explain myself, I find I can't. I will go home and throw what clothes I haven't
donated into a washer and go about my business for a half-hour,
then return to place them in my dryer. They are my clothes. I have
dirtied them, and it seems like pouring salt into a wound to ask
these people to handle my sweaty clothes in addition to paying for
my government's historic lack of good grace.

I know how that sounds. It sounds like a junior high student
who has just read Elie Wiesel's *Night* or witnessed her first example of racism. So be it. If Jesus was here, would he hand his clothes
over to the poor to wash? Or would he just give them the money
he had and try to lighten their burden?

I am embarrassed to talk to the photographer about this, because when I'd mentioned I was having my clothes done, he'd
said nothing. He grew up here and knows the system. He knew
enough to bring large suitcases filled with clothes to leave behind.
I mention to the photographer that despite the awful poverty, people look well dressed. Women favor dresses and skirts (we were
told not to bring pants and certainly no shorts). I watch those who
walk the streets, going nowhere, I suppose, for hours on end, just
walking. The women look like they are going to church. Their
whites, I say, feeling a little stupid, are so *white*. The photographer
tells me that as a Haitian, he was raised to take pride in his appearance. If he even owns a pair of jeans, I have never seen him

in them. He dresses well. And now I realize that keeping their clothes so fresh takes herculean effort.

At night, we hear gunshots in the valley. It is only people celebrating after a soccer game, the guard tells us.

There is no healthcare in Haiti; there is no infrastructure to provide it. If families are able—and 80 percent of the country lives in poverty, 54 percent in what the U.S. government calls "abject poverty"—they must, if a family member falls ill, gather all necessary medical supplies. Say you break your arm falling down a hill. Your family is responsible for assembling—before any work at all can be done—the material necessary for a proper cast, and even the pins, should the doctor decide you need them. These materials must be bought on the street, if you can find them.

Instead, most Haitian families, when someone gets sick, bundle their loved ones into wheelbarrows or carry them on sheets and deposit them outside hospital gates. The hospitals and orphanages are mostly run by churches, and the families trust their loved ones will be taken care of. Whatever minimal supplies or care is available behind those cement walls, it is better than what the families can provide, themselves. They know the Sisters will do what they can, but what they can do also takes herculean effort. A Haitian who lives past fifty-five is a lucky Haitian, indeed.

Early in the week, we visit an orphanage. If ever there is quiet during sharing time, it is that night. In the absence of body fat, the backbone of a malnourished baby simply ends, ridged, at the base of her spine. Without the normal cushion of a baby's bottom, the tailbone feels like a tiny fingernail lightly pressing into your palm. Their arms are cobwebs. Their hair is brittle.

But babies must be held, and the Sisters at the Missionaries of Charity children's hospital haven't the time to get to all the children. It is the same as at the ill-equipped hospitals. Daily, someone drops a baby off at the door. The Sisters will feed and attend to children when a family cannot. Room must be made— sometimes by moving two children onto the same duct-taped crib mattress. Hourly, the Sisters juggle limited medicines and make awful choices: Who to treat? Who to let languish? Inside the gray hospital, the only bright spots are the small tunics the children wear, color-coded by age and room. Small dusty mobiles hang limp in the still air.

Because of the cost, children are limited to one plastic diaper a day. Visiting hours are restricted to ensure that hungry parents don't eat their starving baby's food. The parents do not think they are stealing if they take their sick child's meals. They know that come what may, the Sisters will feed the children, and cadging rice and chicken is nothing in the face of starvation. If a parent cannot eat, the parent cannot work, and then what future awaits their children? Then, too, this is the land of voodoo, and there is a strong belief in curses. Sisters stand guard over the children so that parents don't suffocate a child in an adjoining crib to appease the gods and save their own child.

One baby clings to my dress collar and cries when I lay her down. That is a sign of health in this cursed land. Most babies are too weak to make any noise and those are the ones I cannot forget. Why did I ask to come here? I am angry at myself for pushing for this trip, angry at my bosses for saying yes.

No, that's not true. I'm angry at Haiti.

No. I'm angry at God.

But I can't just go home. If these people can live it, the least I can do is be a witness.

It is all too much, and we are doing too little, and the organizers suggest a trip to the beach that sounds downright sinful. Still, I go, and the photographer returns to the hospital. I feel guilty, but I want one day away from the horror. Later that night, the photographer and I sit off in a corner and he tells me the story of his day. As he stood outside the hospital, a woman came and left her baby—who had been dressed for church, probably in the hope of appealing to the people inside—at the doorstep. The Sisters waited, hoping the mother would change her mind and return for her child, but the mother did not come back and so the nuns finally took the baby inside. When the photographer—the father of a young boy—tells me this story, he is crying. How could someone leave their child like that?

I can't begin to answer him and I don't try. Besides, he knows the answer better than I. He is Haitian.

Nearly half of the country's 8 million people crowd into Port-au-Prince, the capital city, where social services are mostly unavailable, and never mind amenities we take for granted, like clean water and trash pickup. And so it is left to volunteers to sing to and hold babies too sick or weak to do much more than open and shut their eyes in slow motion.

Later, in an open-air hospital, I am speaking fractured Kreyòl to a beautiful woman with sores oozing down her back. Scattered around her are thirty or so beds filled with thirty or so women who are dying of AIDS.

I have studiously tried to learn the language (not a dialect, a language) and I use it whenever I can. So far, children appear to understand me, adults not so much. I know my accent is indecipherable to them, and I imagine I am not using proper tenses—or even proper words. I act out a lot of what I am trying to say, and I have long since given up worrying about looking silly.

We have been told that these women need touch, that the stigma surrounding AIDS in Haiti is even worse than was the stigma surrounding AIDS in America. We have been given plastic bags filled with fingernail polish as an entrée. Even though these women will soon die, they still care about their appearance, we are told. I don't question anything anymore. The woman in front of me is so covered in sores she looks like she's been turned inside out. If she wants lavender nail polish, so be it.

She chooses mauve—a color I like—and I am carefully covering her thick yellow nails with it. I only rarely paint my own nails, so I am not very good at this. Plus, my hands are shaking too much to be accurate.

When I miss a spot, she points to it without comment. And I go back over it with the tiny brush. And then, without warning, my hands stop shaking and I am overcome. No one prepared me for this, and I am, like any good journalist, supposed to be a dispassionate observer, but you cannot go to Haiti and not pick up a starving baby, and here I am holding the hand of a woman who won't see Christmas, and all those books I read mean precisely nothing. Who cares who is in power? (Technically, while I paint the nails of this dying woman, Haiti's leader is in exile in the Central African Republic. The leader, a former priest, was supposed to be the answer for these people. I am angry at him too.)

But who am I? I am only a visitor, and it seems rude to cry, so instead I start humming the beautiful hymn "O, Thou Fount of Every Blessing." In any other circumstance, I cannot hear—much less sing—this song without crying, but not this time. This time it has the effect of a balm.

The woman looks up in surprise, smiles, and starts singing the song in Kreyòl. I stop humming and start singing in English, and after three verses, we are smiling and laughing and I am not missing any more spots on her thick nails.

"I hear 'Haiti,' and I feel like going back to bed," author Tracy Kidder tells me in an interview before I go. His book follows Farmer and his clinic in Haiti's central plateau. I will not meet Farmer, and I will only speak to Kidder, a writer I much respect, on the phone. By the time one of his books is published, Kidder says, he is generally ready to leave his subject, but, he says, he can't leave Haiti.

"I fear for my friends and it's a mess," Kidder said. "Every time I go to Haiti I think it can't get worse and then it is worse. It's heartbreaking. It doesn't make much sense to imagine a stable democracy where large numbers are starving to death and most of the people are illiterate. People need food and clean water and decent shelter, shoes for their children and education. I wouldn't care if a dictator provided those things to the Haitians and it worked."

Everyone's solution for Haiti begins with basics.

We visit the home of Gilbert Wilkens, a medical student whose mother, known throughout the city as Madame Son Son, feeds ninety children a day, from donations from home and abroad. When she started this work several years ago, Madame sent the food home with the children, but older members of the families ate it while the children went without. To prevent that, Madame now has the children finish their meals in front of her. To help, one of the Connecticut team members who has been to Haiti before has arranged to have vitamins sent to Madame's food program. The meal today is hearty: bean sauce, rice, noodles, and chicken. For many, it is their only meal for the day. I watch as the children squeeze next to one another at tables. They wait quietly—how good the food must smell to them—while Madame or Gilbert or one of Gilbert's sisters sings a prayer.

I am walking on wobbly legs now. Haiti's streets aren't level. My head hurts. I can't get the smell out of my nose.

And then we are standing in a nice neighborhood with parks and gated yards, waiting for one of the team members to get information on crafts she will take back to Connecticut to sell in a store. The money will come back to Haiti.

I am starting to look at the world through Haitian eyes. This neighborhood—one of the few with mansions—looks like a good place to beg. Foreigners come here to the Aid to Artisans store to buy Haitian art and crafts. We Americans stand huddled around our two (clean) vans, our pockets heavy with money.

And sure enough, a little boy with pipe cleaner legs runs up and cries, "Blan!" the not-so-complimentary word for foreigner. Even the photographer, the Haitian native whose skin is dark, is a *blan* here. The little boy holds out his hand for gourdes, the Haitian currency.

We've been told that giving money to the street children will only bring on more street children, but how do you say no to a seven-year-old? We get his name—"Ki jan ou rele?" It's

Tiba (TEE-ba), he says. I hand him a roll of money that has been handled so many times it's hard to tell the denomination, and then we stand around and, in the way of people who don't much speak each other's language, we begin to pantomime a conversation. I have gotten very good in Haiti at acting things out, which surprises me because I am all about dignity and the way I have been communicating has been anything but dignified.

But with Tiba, I pretend to kick a soccer ball to him, and he kicks it back. When he scores an imaginary goal, I cheer, and when I score, he cheers. And when we load into the vans and they pull away, Tiba races after us until we round a corner and I can't see him anymore.

"He likes you," one of the travelers says, and I nod.

More than a quarter of Haiti's children are malnourished.

Among children five or younger, 21 percent are underweight and 28 percent suffer from wasting. Ten percent of them won't make it past their fourth birthday. Roughly one in ten is a *restavek* (Kreyòl for "staying with"), a child who works in exchange for room and board, usually under extremely harsh conditions.

We return to the nice neighborhood a few days later, and as we pull through the traffic (there is no way to describe Haitian traffic other than daring), I hear a small voice calling out, "Blan!" and turn to see Tiba running behind the van, waving. He is wearing red-print shorts that are two sizes too large, and struggling to run in shoes that are perhaps three sizes too big. We again stop in front of the crafts store and unload. Tiba runs up, out of breath, and we chat a bit. I hand him some more gourdes, and then he walks with us—the photographer and me—to a nearby park to watch older boys and young men play a spirited game of soccer. There, he shares his wealth with a few of his friends, handing them one gourde each, just less than three cents American. Then it's time to go back to our vans. We stand up, and I pat Tiba on the shoulder and say *bon swa,* goodbye. For a moment, it seems that that will be that, but then he skips up from behind and he puts his fist, the one holding what remains of the money I have given him, into my hand. So I hold his fist and we walk and talk.

Will you come back tomorrow? he asks. (I recognize the word *demen,* tomorrow.)

We are flying out tomorrow, I tell him. I mimic an airplane with my outstretched arms. I have to go home, to my house, *mwen kay.* You won't come back tomorrow? he asks. No, *desole.* I'm sorry.

Tomorrow, I will go back to my life and Tiba and his friends will stay in theirs. We pose for a picture, standing side by side.

I look down, and Tiba is glaring into the camera, arms crossed. So I do the same.

And then I bend to my knees and try to get Tiba to smile.

He does so, but only partly. A kid's got to be tough in Haiti. You want Christ-haunted?

Friends of mine who think they are being helpful—friends who grew up thinking everyone is Catholic—point me toward films they think might appeal to me. The latest is *Jesus Camp,* a 2006 documentary about one pastor's approach to indoctrinating children into the Lord's Army. Becky Fischer—who refers to Muslims as "the enemy"—runs a North Dakota camp for young Pentecostals, and her main weapon to win their little souls to Christ is fear. For all the other characters in the documentary, it is the children—Levi and Rachael and Tory and others—who draw me. They are openhearted and quick to tears and the looks on their faces is heartbreaking when they are shown small plastic fetuses and warned of the evils of abortion.

I watch the DVD in my bedroom, and my anger builds as the children earnestly talk about their charge to go and make disciples in every country.[1] It is riveting and it is painful and I wonder

1. Matthew 28:18–20.

195

how many other recovering fundamentalists—for that is how I am thinking of myself, shaft broken off in me and all—are watching this and feeling their hearts crack open. Because this is so not the point. I did not grow up in the Pentecostal tradition. We believed that gifts of the Holy Spirit ended with the early church, that the usefulness of such gifts had passed,[2] as I'd tried to convince my floating friend, Pat. Nor did we believe in the laying on of hands to heal the sick, nor did we cotton to prophecy. In short, we did not believe in any of the things that make some brands of fundamentalist Christianity so juicy.

But we did believe in indoctrinating—that's a loaded word, isn't it?—children early. Why else would my older brother have felt the call to preach at age twelve? Why else would the other brother have stepped into the pulpit to lead singing at roughly the same age? And why else would I have started teaching Sunday school when the ink was still wet on my baptism Bible? Because we were taught that these were all important and good things to do, and the urgency was that people are dying every day outside of Christ and their souls are shooting straight to hell, and what were we doing about that? We were raised in an individualistic, highly emotional religion, much like Levi, Rachael, and Tory. And I look into their faces—especially dark-haired Rachael's— and see my own and that of my brothers. We believed, we believed, we believed, we believed, and we acted on it, too. We knocked doors because Jesus wanted us to—or so we were told. We grimly skipped school dances because Jesus wanted us to—or so we were told. We gave Jesus our youth because that was what was expected of us. And then when the burden became too great, people like us started drinking, taking drugs, and running as fast as we could from the church. The same way we were frightened into immersing ourselves in that cool baptistery water, we im-

2. 1 Corinthians 13:8.

mersed ourselves in the sins of the flesh, to take that taste of com-munion cracker out of our mouths forever. We'd been lied to. We'd been misled. We were angry.

I pray for Levi, Rachael, and Tory a normal life, a Spirit-filled life that allows them to be in the world, but not of it.[3] And I grimly thank my well-meaning friends for their suggestion that I watch the DVD.

Christ-haunted?

I am interviewing a Hartford performance artist who is a graduate of one of those ex-gay ministries, this one based in Ten-nessee. He'd been raised a Catholic by loving parents in New York, but as he grew and came into the awareness that he is gay, he converted to a Bible-based church, a kind of feeder into Bob Jones University, the South Carolina liberal arts college, a bastion of fundamentalism where the admission form asks if the prospec-tive student has ever consumed alcohol. The performance artist didn't attend Bob Jones. He ended up at New York University, in the theater department, which he left when he realized there were a lot of homosexuals in the theater department and he didn't want to be tempted.

He became a youth leader and a missionary in Africa, but always, his sexual orientation would rise up and bite him and he would, in the vernacular of his fellow believers, act "inappro-priately." He got married, but that didn't work, either. He was found out one day and in a short hour lost his job, his friends, and his wife. He eventually ended up at a Tennessee halfway house for "recovering" homosexuals. He did two stints there, and he emerged both times a homosexual, just as God made him. He talks about his time there in a ninety-minute piece he calls *Doin' Time at the Homo No Mo' Halfway House.* I'd called him around the time evangelical preacher Ted Haggard's patronage of a male

3. John 17:14–15.

prostitute became public, thinking he and I could carve up the good pastor's body in print. I even had a few jokes worked out beforehand.

But then we meet in a Hartford coffee shop, and the performance artist shows more grace than I do. He wants to talk about his faith, and his concern for Haggard, if the pastor thinks he can talk or pray his way out of homosexuality. In the artist's experience, church members want to think of homosexuality as simply an aberration, believing that both Haggard and the artist are heterosexual men who'd simply acted against nature and defiled the temple of the body, that it's a passing thing. Some of us drink too much, some of us have sex with someone of our own gender. Earlier, the artist had written in his blog that Haggard is his brother in shame. Trying to do the right thing when your whole world is telling you that you're fundamentally wrong is just so hard, isn't it?

But God made all of us, gay, straight, and some in between. And as the artist and I talk over lattes, I ask him what he would do if he had five minutes alone with Ted Haggard.

I expected something far different, but as he talks, I start crying. I don't mean to, and I apologize for it because it's off-putting at best to cry during an interview, but he tells the story of the Capernaum woman in Luke 8:43–48 who'd been bleeding for twelve years. She'd spent everything she had in futile attempts to get well, and when she heard of Jesus, she joined the crowd and touched the hem of his garment.

That was all she felt worthy to do, the artist said. Imagine that act, in that time and in that place. A hemorrhaging woman would have been considered unclean. Yet as soon as she touched Jesus's garment, the bleeding stopped and she was whole.

"Who touched me?" Jesus asked, and you can imagine the disciples' annoyance, the artist says. Jesus often got in the way of things running smoothly by spending too much time with the crowds, by stepping off the path, by stopping and listening to a woman.

When Jesus asked this, the woman was frightened and she threw herself in front of him and told him what had happened. Jesus told her that her faith had healed her. And he called her "daughter."

Brother Haggard might draw strength from that story, the artist said. The woman felt only worthy enough to touch Jesus's hem, and she was healed. Her faith healed her.

That is what blindsided me—she felt unworthy, but her faith healed her. That, and the notion that there's a whole army of us, regardless of our orientation, who have been made to understand that we don't fit in and aren't entirely wanted, that we are somehow unclean, unworthy. The performance artist knew that in the eyes of some, his orientation placed him outside God's love, especially according to the believers with whom he once worshipped. And I knew that as a woman, my church did not think me quite worthy of the entirety of God's saving grace. Don't tell me that God had in mind for me a special role. We all know there's no such thing as separate but equal. I either get to walk straight to the throne of God or I don't. There is no halfway and no compromise.

But her faith healed her.

The problem with being outside the church when you spent so much time uncomfortably in it is that when you once and for all step outside, you are on some level acknowledging that those people were right, that you aren't quite worthy. You are a woman without a home, a man without a country. You don't stay and fight, you leave.

I miss the community. I miss the fellowship, and even in my isolation, I miss that feeling of belonging to something—or trying to belong. I know I am wrapping my years in the church in a big bow of nostalgia. So often, I didn't belong. So often, my questions in Sunday school put me on the outside. And yet there was that sense of familiarity. I miss the faces at the table at church dinners. I know the order of worship and I know most of the songs and I miss it to my core. And for years, I let people tell me that I didn't belong and the sad fact is that I believed them.

When I ask the performance artist if he considers himself a Christian, he answers, without hesitation, "Yes." And he explains what a radical act that is, that for so many people with whom he matured he is so far outside the grace of God, even his mouthing the word "Christian" would be blasphemy. And yet he takes it as his own. He is a Christian, and those people who would send him straight to hell? They don't get a vote. It is all I can do not to cry again. What a radical idea, to claim membership with the larger body when the body doesn't want you.

I sometimes think the answer is for us outsiders to start our own church. It has to have a little bit of substance (and nothing cutting-edge like a praise dance team. I'm sorry. I'm only able to walk partway on this, I guess.). We need a community of believers, but most of us don't want to give up our Sunday mornings with the newspaper, or our hikes, or our time spent in the kitchen preparing the week's meals. We must create our own means of making a worshipful community, so let's start with a cookbook. We can call it the Non-Church Auxiliary Cookbook for Heathens. Submit your recipes to me. All credit due will be credit given. If your recipe has a little story behind it, include that, as well. And there has to be music in our new church that includes close harmony and scary lyrics and a proud gaggle of men who sing bass and come in and shake the timbers on the chorus. There has to be music to remind us of those camp meetings when the itinerant preacher who had nothing to lose sweated into the microphone and shorted out the lights.

There has to be passion. And fear, but a happy kind of fear, the kind of thrilling fear you feel on a roller coaster.

Christ-haunted?

I interview Letha Dawson Scanzoni, coauthor of *What God Has Joined Together: A Christian Case for Gay Marriage*. I am writing a lot more than the opposition wants to read about the need for extending the same rights to same-sex couples now enjoyed by opposite-sex ones. I am disheartened that my state of Connecticut has stopped just shy of full human rights and instead has delivered civil unions—Marriage Lite, all the ceremony but not all of the rights—to same-sex couples. Civil unions in Connecticut is a political move and I understand that, but what I don't understand is people's rabid opposition to homosexuals themselves. I got over my early prejudice and I expect no less from everyone else. And so my column is devoted quite a lot to same-sex marriage and I am a frequent topic of discussion (I hesitate to say "target," because honestly? Most of the people who disagree with me are reasonable about it) on Connecticut-based blogs. I talk to Scanzoni because of the book she cowrote with David G. Myers, a Michigan psychologist. It is a weighty Christian argument in favor of homosexual rights, particularly in the realm of marriage. Much of my discussions with naysayers revolve around cherry-picked verses meant to send homosexuals straight to hell—only the verses don't send homosexuals to hell. On the phone, Scanzoni is a lively and smart interview and the column runs and I move on to the next big thing, as I'm sure she does, as well.

But months later, she e-mails me to congratulate me on yet another in my series of columns that I joke to friends should be compiled into a book titled, *You Leave Them Queers Alone.* I e-mail back and she thoughtfully sends a packet that includes the updated version of her homosexual-rights book, a stack of *Christian Feminism Today* newsletters, and the third edition of her and Nancy A. Hardesty's book, *All We're Meant to Be: Biblical Feminism for Today.* The women had tried for years to get a publisher after writing the book in 1974, and *Christianity Today* magazine recently named it one of the "top 50 books that have shaped evangelicals." My favorite chapter is: "It All Started with Eve." I read the book in great gulps and it is like cool water racing down a parched throat. Scanzoni and Hardesty, who helped start the

Evangelical and Ecumenical Women's Caucus, have plowed the field that I am just now beginning to survey. It is beautiful work that speaks directly to me. In one newsletter, biblical scholar Virginia Ramey Mollenkott talks about growing up fundamentalist and then returning later, with a new perspective, to the Scriptures of her youth. The sum of my struggle is contained in something she said about reading the Bible: "I was wearing fundamentalist blinders when I read the Bible," she said, "and was afraid to take them off." And it's contained in a lively essay by Anne Eggebroten, research scholar at the UCLA Center for the Study of Women: "Sometimes you've just got to laugh. As feminists in churches still controlled by men, our choices are to laugh, cry, or pray, and I find myself rotating among these options on a daily basis."

To the activities included in my own rotation, I would add "pound the walls with my fists." And I left the church. Do I even have a vote anymore?

Christ-haunted?

I remember the first newspaper reader who called me a liberal. I was stunned into silence. I had never thought of myself as particularly political—neither liberal nor conservative. The reader was responding to—you can't make this stuff up—an essay on hanging bedclothes out on the line to dry. I am tired, she sniffed in her letter, of you politicizing everything. Up to that point, I hadn't realized I was doing that, but it was at a time when I was withdrawing from the church of my girlhood, disenchanted with all the messages save for a select few I learned in Sunday school. Life should be fair, and when it isn't, those of us who end up with bigger piles should share. Jesus never meant for us to be mistrustful of one another, and he certainly never encouraged us to hate. While I was backing off from teaching Sunday school in the small church of Christ I'd found after I moved east, I was reading my Bible more closely. I might not grab a microphone at the pulpit and start sweating, but I would use my bully pulpit at my newspaper.

•

No, I do not see my journalism as a mission, nor would I use it to call the sinners to the Cross—nothing scary like that. Instead, I would use it as a forum to discuss ethics and values—and not just Judeo-Christian ones. I figured Jesus wouldn't mind. He'd always been pretty open-minded that way, from what I'd discovered.

A friend is the DJ for a folk music show on a radio station based at the University of Connecticut. I've started tuning in early because the show before hers, a bluegrass one, ends its Sunday broadcast with a half-hour of old-time gospel. I'm listening to a quartet of men swoop and whirl and I'm singing along, being that I am alone in the house. My children are grown and gone—one to college and the other to his own big-boy apartment a half-hour away. My husband is gone for the day to visit the son in college. I am pretty sure no one will walk in on my private choir practice, and these days, when I'm home alone, I'm usually singing. It is my guilty pleasure, to harmonize at the top of my lungs, to gospel tunes—especially the ones performed a cappella. Forgive me for that. You can run at full speed from your fundamentalist up-bringing, but it's going to catch up with you, regardless.

I am on a particularly ear-splitting note on "A Beautiful Life" when I am struck by a scary thought. What if I've been wrong all along, and the Holy Spirit does still come upon us heathens, and what if it comes upon me unexpectedly one day and I start speaking in tongues and laying my hands on people to heal them? What if the Christianity I have walked away from was wrong in the first place, and the right one is actually a more charismatic one, one that can't be safely contained in a three-times-a-week visit to a quiet church? What if real Christianity isn't as polite as I'd like it to be? After all, I have a friend who went the reverse way and ended up an Episcopalian priest.

Nah. God would not mess with me like that. Would she?

After all this navel-gazing, anger, and resignation, surely the

Christianity that's waiting for me is the Christianity Jesus and I work out between us, like two old friends who know the topics to avoid and the topics to embrace. And what if, in the end, I'm allowed that one look backward over my whole life and my reaction is—as I expect it to be—Oh. Is *that* all that was? Jaysus. Oh. Sorry.

And then one cold, dark, New England winter morning, I wake up, just like that. I am dreaming something weird about Justin Timberlake's grandmother (whose name, in my dream, is Mrs. Berman[4]). I don't ever think about Justin Timberlake in my waking life, and it is bothering me even as I dream that I am thinking about him in my sleeping one. His grandmother seems like a lovely woman, but she shows me a picture of a man in a morning coat and a white tie and as I draw closer, I get nervous that the picture will be scary. I have no idea why I'm dreaming this, so I wake up. I have learned to do that after a childhood spent battling bad dreams. When the monster closes in, I wake up.

The moon is full in the skylight in my bedroom and I lay there looking up at it. My husband is next to me, snoring gently, not enough to wake me and not enough to keep me from going back to sleep, either.

And then there is a quiet voice, and it says, "It was the wrong Jesus."

At first, I think that maybe my dream is continuing, and it's taken a strange turn, from Mrs. Berman to Jesus. But then I realize the voice is mine. I am speaking out loud in my bed—quietly, so as not to wake my husband. Apropos of nothing in that weird dream, I realize: All those years ago? I dated the wrong Jesus.

Or, rather, the entity I dated through high school and college and into my early adult years was emphatically not Jesus. It was someone's idea of Jesus, but not the real one. I dated the wrong

---

4. In fact, according to my *People* magazine, at least one of Justin Timberlake's grandmothers is named Sadie Bomar. I know this because she publicly gave her opinion as to his choice of life mates.

one. I gave my heart and my soul—literally—to a construct that had only a small basis in fact.

The real Jesus wouldn't have worried if I spoke out in Sunday school. He might have expected it—demanded it, even. He tended to gravitate to mouthy women who were willing to buck convention and pick up and follow him, social mores be damned. They saw in him something they saw in absolutely nothing else in their lives, and so they followed.

The real Jesus wouldn't have loved me less because of my gender. He most likely would have shown me a kind of understanding I wouldn't have received from many other people in my life. He would have been OK with the quirks and the really mean parts of me I try to ignore. He would have listened to my bad and weird dreams. He wouldn't have demanded I step into a box and nail that sucker shut.

The real Jesus wouldn't have weighed me down with rules— a list of do's and don'ts that serve no real purpose.

The real Jesus would have allowed me to mature naturally and in my own good time.

The real Jesus would have loved me for me.

The real Jesus would have had a sense of humor about the whole thing, goddammit.

I tuck myself back in, but I don't go to sleep. Instead, I lay there in my warm, comfy bed and I laugh out loud.

Darlin', I think to myself, *What took you so long?*

Oh, it doesn't end there. It can't. I am still, at heart, a floater. I am still seeking. I will arm-wrestle with God for a while longer and then no more. In the end, I am counting on her forgiveness and I imagine I'm not alone in this. I ask for forgiveness for my hardheadedness. I ask forgiveness for the mistakes I've made in my long and complicated walk. And I ask forgiveness for this:

The farthest I can get on a good day is this: I believe God. God, I believe.

ACKNOWLEDGMENTS

You can't write a book by yourself—at least I couldn't. So I'd like to thank, in no particular order: the fine folks at Hartford Seminary, who made me think; Amy Caldwell, editor supreme, who made sense of things when I simply couldn't; Joanna Green, ditto; Melissa Dobson, who read this so carefully it frightened me; Doug Anderson, Susanne Davis, Leslie Johnson, and Wally Lamb, who saw this three pages in and were so encouraging, I kept going; Helen Ubiñas, who found me a wonderful publisher; Tina Jeter, Kim Harty, Judy Folger, and Helen, again, who kept asking "So? How's the book?"; a string of Sunday school teachers at the Fourth and Forest church of Christ, who pointed me in the general direction; my brothers, who taught me to drive, field grounders, and tell jokes; my little sister, who continues to teach me everything else; the Rileys, who took me in when they didn't have to; Grandma Marrs, who should have been in charge; Jesus, who always pretty much was; my sons, Ryan and Sam, who taught me more about unconditional love than I could ever teach them; and finally, Frank, my best friend, my severest critic, and the smartest man in the room. George Bailey, I will love you till the day I die. And, if it is possible, even further.

ABOUT MY SOURCES

I am influenced by everything from scholarly works to bad '70s television. This just serves my thesis that even if you claim agnosticism, theology will find you. Sources that I've quoted from directly are mentioned in the text, with bibliographic information given here. Other sources given served as inspiration or proved important to me in developing my thinking, but the list is not inclusive.

Chapter 1—The Devil's in an Air Bubble
My information comes from the Holy Bible—several versions, including the dusty old King James—and *Tiger Beat* magazine, as well as the lessons I learned in more hours than I can count in Sunday-morning and Wednesday-evening Bible classes, as well as a glorious week spent each summer at Green Valley Bible Camp in Rogers, Arkansas.

Chapter 2—I Don't Want to Preach, But . . .
What I know of the Torah comes in large part from George Robinson's *Essential Torah: A Complete Guide to the Five Books of Moses* (New York: Random House, 2006).

For the one-true-church discussion, in 2000, then-cardinal Joseph Alois Ratzinger (now Pope Benedict XVI) released *Dominus Iesus,* a document that allowed that at least some Christians baptized outside the Roman Catholic faith are at least in communion with Christ, albeit imperfectly.

For the history of fundamentalism and evangelicalism, see Ernest R. Sandeen, *The Roots of Fundamentalism: British and American Millennialism, 1800–1830* (Chicago: University of Chicago, 1970); William S. Banowsky, *The Mirror of a Movement: Churches of Christ As Seen Through the Abilene Christian College Lectureship* (Dallas: Christian Publishing, 1965); Richard Quebedeaux, *The Worldly Evangelicals: Has Success Spoiled America's Born Again Christians?* (New York: Harper and Rowe, 1978). And that key primary source, Milton and Lymon Stewart's *The Fundamentals: A Testimony to the Truth…Compliments of Two Christian Laymen* (Chicago: Testimony, 1910–15).

Anyone who studies Christian fundamentalism needs George M. Marsden as a guide, particularly the latest edition of his *Fundamentalism and American Culture* (New York: Oxford University Press, 2006), as well as James Barr's *Fundamentalism* (Philadelphia: Westminster Press, 1978). Add to these Steve Brouwer, Paul Gifford, and Susan D. Rose, *Exporting the American Gospel: Global Christian Fundamentalism* (New York: Routledge, 1996); Vincent Crapanzo, *Serving the Word: Literalism in America from the Pulpit to the Bench* (New York: New Press, 2001); and John H. Simpson, "Moral Issues and Status Politics," in *The New Christian Right: Mobilization and Legitimization,* edited by Robert C. Liebman and Robert Wuthnow (New York: Aldine, 1983).

I also referred to Gary Wills, *What Paul Meant* (New York: Viking, 2006). The H. L. Mencken quotes are taken from *H. L. Mencken on Religion,* edited by S. T. Yoshi (Amherst, MA: Prometheus, 2002).

Chapter 3 — Knocking Doors for Jesus

Here's where things get a little weird. I relied on both Charles Dickens's *A Christmas Carol* and the *CIA World Factbook* for images (Jacob Marley and his chain) and information contained in this chapter. You are warned. I also went back to Crapanzo's *Serving the Word: Literalism in America from the Pulpit to the Bench.*

Chapter 4—A Good Christian Woman

Is there anyone who hasn't read Anita Diamant's wonderful *The Red Tent* (New York: St. Martin's, 1997)? For historical perspective, I relied on *Discourse on Woman,* by Lucretia Mott (Philadelphia: W.P. Kildare, 1869), and "Declaration of Sentiments and Resolutions," Elizabeth Cady Stanton's seminal 1848 document, widely available online and at the National Women's History Museum in Seneca Falls. I relied, as well, on *The Woman's Bible,* edited by Stanton (New York: European, 1895–98). I quote from Maureen Fitzgerald's introduction to a 1993 edition of this source, published by Northeastern University Press. See also Katherine C. Bushnell's *God's Word to Women,* published in 1923.

I'd also recommend, for a modern perspective, Anne McGrew Bennett's "Overcoming the Biblical and Traditional Subordination of Women," in *Feminist Theological Ethics: A Reader,* edited by Lois K. Daly (Louisville, KY: Westminster John Knox Press, 1994). This book is the source of my knowledge of the original Hebrew and God's intent with regard to women.

Chapter 5—The Theology of Softball

Most helpful was Karen Blumenthal's *Let Me Play: The Story of Title IX: The Law That Changed the Future of Girls in America* (New York: Simon and Schuster, 2005), and Drucilla Cornell's *At the Heart of Freedom: Feminism, Sex & Equality* (Princeton, NJ: Princeton University Press, 1998).

Chapter 6—A Woman's Role

In order, I relied on: Robert William Fogel, *The Fourth Great Awakening & the Future of Egalitarianism* (Chicago: University of Chicago Press, 2000); Nancy T. Ammerman, "North American Protestant Fundamentalism, Fundamentalisms Observed," in *Media, Culture, and the Reli-*

gious Right, edited by Linda Kintz and Julia Lesage (Minneapolis: University of Minnesota Press, 1998); Catherine Clinton, *The Other Civil War: American Women in the Nineteenth Century* (New York: Hill and Wang, 1999); Ann Braude, *Radical Spirits: Spiritualism and Women's Rights in Nineteenth-Century America* (Boston: Beacon Press, 2001); Vivian Gornick, *Essays in Feminism* (New York: Harper & Row, 1931); James Davison Hunter, *American Evangelicalism: Conservative Religion and the Quandary of Modernity* (New Brunswick, NJ: Rutgers University Press, 1983), and Walter Rauschenbusch, *A Theology for the Social Gospel* (New York: Macmillan, 1917).

See also the spectacular Karen Armstrong, *The Battle for God* (New York: Alfred A. Knopf, 2000); Walter Russell Mead, "Religion & U.S. Foreign Policy: How the Evangelical Boom Is Remaking the Country's Politics at Home and Abroad" *Foreign Affairs* (Sept./Oct. 2006); Michael Kazin, *The Populist Persuasion: An American History* (Ithaca, NY: Cornell University Press, 1998); Nancy F. Cott, *The Grounding of Modern Feminism* (New Haven, CT: Yale University Press, 1987); Harvard University, Newman Library, Digital Collections, "An American Family: The Beecher Tradition: Catharine Beecher," available at http://ocp.hul. harvard.edu; Ellen Carol DuBois, *Woman Suffrage and Women's Rights* (New York: New York University Press, 1998); Frances E. Willard, *Woman in the Pulpit* (Boston: D. Lothrop, 1889); Carolyn Gifford, ed., *Writing Out My Heart: Selections from the Journal of Frances E. Willard, 1855–96* (Chicago: University of Illinois Press, 1995); back to Drucilla Cornell, *At the Heart of Freedom; Feminism, Sex & Equality*; Ann Belford Ulanov and Barry Ulanov, *Religion and the Unconscious* (Philadelphia: Westminster, 1975); Elizabeth Mitchell, "An Odd Break with the Human Heart," in *To Be Real: Telling the Truth and Changing the Face of Feminism* (New York: Anchor, 1995); Mary Potter Engel, "Evil, Sin, and Violation of the Vulnerable," in *Lift Every Voice: Constructing Christian Theologies from the Underside,* edited by Susan B. Thistlethwaite and Mary Potter Engel (San Francisco: Harper & Row, 1990); back to *Exporting the American Gospel: Global Christian Fundamentalism* (New York: Routledge, 1996); Susan D. Rose, "Christian Fundamentalism: Patriarchy, Sexuality and Human Rights," in *Religious Fundamentalisms and the Human Rights of Women,* edited by Courtney W. Howland (New

York: Macmillan, 1999); Rosemary Radford Ruether and Eleanor Mc-Laughlin, eds., *Women of Spirit: Female Leadership in the Jewish and Christian Tradition* (New York: Simon & Schuster, 1974).

See also Geoffrey C. Ward and Kenneth Burns, *Not for Ourselves Alone: The Story of Elizabeth Cady Stanton and Susan B. Anthony* (New York: Alfred A. Knopf, 2000); Walter Lippmann, *Drift and Mastery: An Attempt to Diagnose the Current Unrest* (New York: M. Kennerly, 1914); Christian Smith, *American Evangelicalism: Embattled and Thriving* (Chicago: University of Chicago Press, 1998), and last—but certainly not least—Martin E. Marty and R. Scott Appleby, *The Glory and the Power: The Fundamentalist Challenge to the Modern World* (Boston: Beacon Press, 1992).

Jesus, I hope I didn't forget anyone.

Chapter 7—A Scary God

Searching for the Wrong-Eyed Jesus (2003) is available at any DVD rental establishment worth its salt.

My take on Julian of Norwich was largely inspired by *The Life of the Soul: The Wisdom of Julian of Norwich,* translated by Edmund Colledge, O.S.A., and James Walsh, S.J. (Mahwah, NJ: Paulist Press, 1996). See also *The Revelation of Divine Love in Sixteen Showings Made to Dame Julian of Norwich*, translated with an introduction by M. L. del Mastro (Liguori, MO: Triumph Books, 1994).

Also of help to me was Lisa Sergio, *Jesus and Woman: An Exciting Discovery of What He Offered Her* (McLean, VA: EPM, 1975); Elisabeth Schüssler Fiorenza, *In Memory of Her: A Feminist Theological Reconstruction of Christian Origins* (New York: Crossroad, 1994); Joyce Hollyday, *Clothed with the Sun: Biblical Women, Social Justice, and Us* (Louisville, KY: Westminster John Knox Press, 1994); Judith Antonelli, "The Goddess Myth," *Utne Reader* (Nov./Dec. 1997); Miriam Therese Winter, *The Gospel According to Mary: A New Testament for Women* (New York: Crossroad, 1993); and Winter's *The Chronicles of Noah and Her Sisters: Genesis and Exodus According to Women* (New York: Crossroad, 1995).

Chapter 8— The Reluctant Female

Information about evangelicals cutting loose was gleaned from a *New York Times Magazine* article by Mark Oppenheimer, "The First Dance: One small Christian college finds that there may be some redemption in being footloose after all," January 28, 2007. Quoted in the text is Mary Wollstonecraft's *A Vindication of the Rights of Woman* (reprint, New York: Alfred A. Knopf, 1992). I also found helpful Karen Jo Torjesen's *When Women Were Priests: Women's Leadership in the Early Church & the Scandal of Their Subordination in the Rise of Christianity* (San Francisco: HarperSanFrancisco, 1995); Thomas Cahill's *Mysteries of the Middle Ages: The Rise of Feminism, Science, and Art from the Cults of Catholic Europe* (New York: Nan A. Talese, 2006); Barbara Ehrenreich's *Dancing in the Streets: A History of Collective Joy* (New York: Henry Holt & Co., 2006); and Tony Campolo's *Letters to a Young Evangelical: The Art of Mentoring* (New York: Perseus, 2006).

Chapter 9— Still, Small Voice

See Ralph C. Wood, *Flannery O'Connor and the Christ-Haunted South* (Grand Rapids, MI: William. B. Eerdmans, 2004); again Robert William Fogel, *The Fourth Great Awakening & the Future of Egalitarianism;* Bob Edgar, *Middle Church: Reclaiming the Moral Values of the Faithful Majority from the Religious Right* (New York: Simon & Schuster, 2006); John Danforth, *Faith and Politics: How the "Moral Values" Debate Divides America and How to Move Forward Together* (New York: Viking, 2006); and Jay Bakker and Marc Brown, "What the Hell Happened to Christianity?" CNN.com, December 14, 2006.

Chapter 10— Water Jugs

On this chapter I got massive help from: Elisabeth Moltmann-Wendel, *The Women around Jesus* (New York: Crossroad, 1982); Susan Haskins, *Mary Magdalene: Myth and Metaphor* (New York: Harcourt, Brace, 1993); Alicia Craig Faxon, *Women and Jesus* (Philadelphia: Pilgrim Press, 1973); again, the glorious Karen Armstrong, this time with *A History of God: The 4,000-Year Quest of Judaism, Christianity, and Islam* (New

York: Ballantine, 1994), and Carla Ricci, *Mary Magdalene and Many Others: Women Who Followed Jesus* (Minneapolis: Fortress, 1994).

See, too, John Dominic Crossan, *The Historical Jesus: The Life of a Mediterranean Jewish Peasant* (San Francisco: HarperSanFrancisco, 1993); Miriam Therese Winter, again, *The Chronicle of Noah and Her Sisters;* Andrew Greeley, *Jesus: A Meditation on His Stories and His Relationships with Women* (New York: Forge, 2007); Graham N. Stanton, *The Gospels and Jesus,* 2d ed. (New York: Oxford University Press, 2002); Ann Belford Ulanov, *The Female Ancestors of Christ* (Boston: Shambhala, 1993); William E. Phipps, *The Sexuality of Jesus* (Cleveland: Pilgrim, 1996); Letha Dawson Scanzoni and Nancy A. Hardesty, *All We're Meant to Be: Biblical Feminism for Today* (Grand Rapids, MI: William B. Eerdmans, 1992); Ben Witherington III, *Women in the Ministry of Jesus: A Study of Jesus' Attitudes to Women and Their Roles as Reflected in His Earthly Life* (London: Cambridge University Press, 1984); Reta Halteman Finger, "Finding Our Sisters," *Other Side* (Nov./Dec. 1996); Stephen Charles Mott, "Jesus' Attack on a Restriction of Women," *Christian Social Action* (June 1996); W. H. C. Frend, *The Early Church* (Minneapolis: Fortress, 1982); Jana Opecenska, "Women at the Cross at Jesus' Burial and after the Resurrection," *Reformed Word* (March 1997); Elisabeth Moltmann-Wendel and Jurgen Moltmann, *Humanity in God* (New York: Pilgrim, 1983); back to *Women of Spirit: Female Leadership in the Jewish and Christian Tradition;* Luke Timothy Johnson, *The Writings of the New Testament: An Interpretation* (Norwich, U.K.: SCM Press, 2003); Elisabeth Schüssler Fiorenza, again, *In Memory of Her: A Feminist Theological Reconstruction of Christian Origins*; Anne Jensen, *God's Self-Confident Daughters: Early Christianity and the Liberation of Women* (Louisville, KY: Westminster John Knox, 1996); and Sandra M. Schneiders, *The Revelatory Text: Interpreting the New Testament as Sacred Scripture* (San Francisco: HarperSanFrancisco, 1991); and Stephen Prothero, *Religious Literacy: What Every American Needs to Know—And Doesn't* (San Francisco: HarperSanFrancisco, 2007).

Chapter 11 — Jesus Haunts Me, This I Know

I had diverse help on this, starting with the *CIA World Factbook* on Haiti, available at https://www.cia.gov. I also consulted Tracy Kidder's *Mountains Beyond Mountains: The Quest of Dr. Paul Farmer, a Man Who Would Cure the World* (New York: Random House, 2003); Paul Farmer's (with foreword by Jonathan Kozol and introduction by Noam Chomsky) *The Uses of Haiti,* 3d ed. (Monroe, ME: Common Courage Press, 2005); Paul Farmer's *Pathologies of Power: Health, Human Rights, and the New War on the Poor* (Berkeley: University of California Press, 2003); Frances Temple, *Taste of Salt: A Story of Modern Haiti* (New York: Harper-Collins, 1992); E. Wade Davis, *The Serpent and the Rainbow* (New York: Simon and Schuster, 1985); Marin Ros, *Night of Fire: The Black Napoleon and the Battle for Haiti* (Cambridge, MA: Da Capo Press, 1994), and Graham Greene, *The Comedians* (New York: Penguin Classics, 1966).

In addition, I consulted David G. Myers and Letha Dawson Scanzoni's *What God Has Joined Together? A Christian Case for Gay Marriage* (New York: HarperOne, 2005) and, again, Scanzoni and Nancy A. Hardesty's *All We're Meant to Be: Biblical Feminism for Today.*

Quoted in the chapter are Virginia Ramey Mollenkott, "Feminism and Evangelicalism," *EEWC Update* 29, no. 1 (spring 2005), and Anne Eggebroten, "Of Buttons, Baptists, and Don Quixotes," *Christian Feminism Today* 30, no. 3 (fall 2006).